ANNOTATED TEACHER'S EDITION

Mathematics
Reading Strategies

Program Consultant
Dr. Kate Kinsella
San Francisco State University
San Francisco, California

GLOBE FEARON
Pearson Learning Group

Program Consultant
Dr. Kate Kinsella
Dept. of Secondary Education and
Step to College Program
San Francisco State University
San Francisco, CA

Consultant
John Edwin Cowen, Ed.D.
Assistant Professor, Education/Reading
Program Coordinator, Graduate M.A.T./
Elementary Education
School of Education
Fairleigh Dickinson University
Teaneck, NJ

Supervising Editor: Lynn W. Kloss
Senior Editor: Reneé E. Beach
Editorial Assistant: Jennifer Watts
Writer: Sandra Widener
Production Editor: Laura Benford-Sullivan
Cover and Interior Design: Sharon Scannell
Electronic Page Production: Linda Bierniak, Phyllis Rosinsky
Manufacturing Supervisor: Mark Cirillo

ISBN: 0-130-23792-2
Printed in the United States of America
4 5 6 7 8 9 10   06 05 04 03 02

1-800-321-3106
www.pearsonlearning.com

Contents

Foreword by Dr. Kate Kinsella

How does the reading task change as students move from elementary school to middle school?

In elementary classrooms, instruction is focused on helping students "learn to read." On the threshold of adolescence, students experience a quantum leap in moving from the carefully monitored narrative reading tasks of their elementary language arts instruction to the conceptually and linguistically dense texts they must independently navigate in their middle school coursework. Beyond fifth grade, students are routinely expected to not only tackle core works of literature, but also more frequently "read to learn" from expository texts that explain central lesson concepts and processes in diverse subject areas.

Classroom experience and educational research suggest that most students have few effective strategies that they can apply to learning from expository texts. Middle school and high school students—whether high achieving or less prepared—need developmental content literacy instruction to extend and refine the reading and writing abilities they often bring from their elementary education.

How do you define "content literacy"?

McKenna and Robinson (1990) define content literacy as the ability to use reading and writing to acquire new content in a specific subject area. A student who is content literate has a heightened awareness and can use the structure and features of distinct informational texts, such as a newspaper article or a research report, and knows how to read in strategic ways to obtain knowledge from them. In addition, this text-wise reader makes a critical distinction between reading and analyzing an expository text in order to identify critical information to be learned, as opposed to later mastering the material by organizing it in some meaningful form of study notes.

In contrast, less sophisticated readers may possess considerable prior knowledge about the Civil War yet may lack the requisite literacy tools to confidently read and learn from a relevant textbook chapter or primary source document. They struggle to focus their attention appropriately and identify more significant information within a chapter section, often because they are unfamiliar with the function of organizational features such as an introduction, subheadings, topic sentences, and transitional expressions. Lacking this expository "text-wiseness," they tend to view all assigned reading as some form of "story," and so they predictably start at the chapter beginning and then progress slowly and aimlessly until they lose both stamina and motivation.

How can all teachers help expand students' content literacy?

Educators in every subject area should have as a primary instructional goal teaching students *how* to learn and not just *what* to learn. It is unrealistic and irresponsible to expect students in upper-elementary classrooms and beyond to adopt—through osmosis, incidental instruction, or voluntary pleasure reading—an informed and flexible approach to reading and learning from curricula in distinct fields of study. Young learners should not be abandoned to their own relatively unproductive devices to develop critical competencies for higher education and the challenging Information Age arena.

As interdisciplinary colleagues, we must therefore strive to move beyond the rhetoric of inclusive, multicultural education and explore collaboratively and comprehensively what is truly involved in educational access and equity. Teachers in reading classrooms and content classrooms alike can indeed make concrete strides in this direction by ensuring that all learners are granted challenging, yet accessible core reading curricula, as well as the cognitive secrets and strategies of content-literate students. By making explicit the potent strategies used by competent students to read, study, and learn across the subject areas, we will be able to successfully empower all students.

How can the Reading Strategies *series help students read to learn?*

The *Reading Strategies* series is an invaluable resource for teachers who have been searching for curricular guidance in crafting a dynamic course to prepare young readers for the literacy demands of content-area classrooms. Several features of this informational reading and study skills series make it a particularly appealing and pedagogically sound curriculum choice. The eclectic array of topical crosscurricular selections will be seen as an instructional boon to all teachers who have struggled in vain to compile a viable portfolio of engaging, clearly written, and unintimidating informational texts. Novice readers in the content areas benefit from sustained practice with relatively brief yet challenging expository selections, which pique their curiosity in the subject matter while providing a productive vehicle for strategy application. Less well-prepared students, who have habitually approached textbook assignments with trepidation, are in particular need of routine rather than periodic success with informational reading in all of the core subject areas.

This series further encourages reticent academic readers by introducing a manageable and developmentally appropriate tool kit of strategies for learning from informational texts. Unlike recreational narrative texts, informational text assignments typically require a more active and focused stance, multiple readings, and some form of synthesized notes for study and review. As students work through the book, they are exposed to an accessible repertoire of strategies for reading to learn, and they are given ample opportunities to apply each strategy to new literacy tasks.

The *Reading Strategies* series can serve as the vital curricular scaffold for a course focusing upon early content literacy development. However, it requires teachers to become inspiring reading coaches who can provide a compelling rationale for each strategy, dynamic modeling, and abundant encouragement and praise at every stage.

About the *Reading Strategies* series

The *Reading Strategies* series has been designed to teach students those strategies that will help them comprehend language arts material. The students who will most benefit from these books are students who may be able to understand individual words but have difficulty assembling ideas into a meaningful whole.

Why Use *Reading Strategies*? The strategies taught in the Student Edition have been adapted and, in some cases, created to solve problems students frequently have with reading comprehension. All have as their goal giving students those tools they can use when they approach any reading assignment, especially the often-challenging material in content-area texts.

The Steps of the Strategies This four-step approach helps students become actively involved with their reading.

> **Step 1: Preview.** Students look over what they will read to create a context for learning and to focus their attention.
>
> **Step 2: Read.** Students read actively, thinking about what they know and looking for answers to questions they have generated.
>
> **Step 3: Take Notes.** Students take notes on what they have read, identifying major points and supporting details, and reflecting on what they have learned.
>
> **Step 4: Review.** Students review what they have read by writing a summary or practicing what they have learned in some other way.

The Student Edition In the Student Edition,

- Students use a step-by-step process to learn the four strategies.
- Students apply the strategies to selections in a specific content area.
- Students learn skills for understanding words in context in Vocabulary Strategies, a vocabulary handbook.

Using the Student Edition The Student Edition supports students in learning to use reading strategies. Included are:

- Unit Openers that present the strategies students will find in each content area.
- Strategy Tips that make suggestions for using the strategy effectively.
- Graphic organizers that have student-created notes and space for students to add their own notes.
- Vocabulary Tips that offer clues for understanding the meaning of new words.
- Test Tips that help students understand how to answer test questions.
- Unit Reviews that can be used as informal reviews or as practice tests.
- Vocabulary Exercises that students can apply to all of their assignments.
- Additional readings at the end of the text that give students an opportunity for further review.
- A Strategy Quick Review that serves as a brief refresher.

Using this Annotated Teacher's Edition This Annotated Teacher's Edition reinforces the lessons in the Student Edition. Included are:

- Answers at point of use.
- Detailed Lesson Plans for teaching and modeling the strategy lessons.
- Lesson Notes for all the lessons in the Student Edition as well as Vocabulary Strategies.
- Internet Connections to help students extend their knowledge of the topic.
- A complete Answer Key for the Student Edition.
- Reproducible Graphic Organizers to support all the strategies.

Teaching Reading to Learn

Teaching Tip

Choose a selection from your classroom text to use with the following techniques.

The following pages contain suggestions for teaching students how to read to learn. To apply any of the strategies introduced in the *Reading Strategies* series, students need to engage actively with text before, during, and after they read. Students should practice these behaviors until they become automatic. Because these behaviors are simply activities that effective readers do without thinking, they can be taught successfully by both reading teachers and content-area teachers.

To successfully comprehend text, students should:

Prereading	• set a purpose for reading. • tap prior knowledge. • preview and predict what they will read.
During Reading	• look for key concepts and main ideas. • make inferences (hypotheses) and check them. • address comprehension problems as they arise.
Postreading	• confirm key concepts and main ideas. • reread if necessary. • review what they have read.

Prereading

Activities students engage in before reading help them prepare to learn new information. Preparing to read helps students incorporate what they read into their existing knowledge.

During prereading, students should:
- identify key terms.
- assess the level of difficulty and length of the selection.
- gain a general sense of the topic and major subtopics.
- understand text organization.
- determine how this information relates to what they already know.

Here are some active learning behaviors that students should initiate before reading:

Consider why they are reading and create a plan for reading
This task requires students to think about why they are reading. What was the purpose of the assignment? If students are unclear about this, they need to find out why they are reading.

Next, students should look at the assignment to get a sense of how long and how difficult it is. Can they read the assignment in one session, or should they break it into several sessions?

Think about what they know about the topic
Students who engage with the text create a scaffold for learning. When

they bring prior knowledge to bear on their readings, students become involved with the text.

Preview the selection

When students preview, they think about what they already know about a topic and get a general idea of what they will learn. Students should:

- **Look at the title and subheadings.** These signal important ideas and usually hint at text organization.

- **Look at other graphic aids.** These include words within the text in italic or bold type, which may be vocabulary words or new concepts. Students should also look at aids such as maps and illustrations in the text.

- **Read the first and last paragraphs.** These often contain the thesis or major points of the reading. Remind students to connect what they are previewing with what they already know about the topic.

- **Read the first sentence or topic sentence of each paragraph.** Often, the main point of a paragraph is found at the beginning.

- **Get an idea of the text structure.** If students understand how the text is organized—for example, chronologically or in cause-and-effect form—they will be better able to follow the text.

During and Just-After Reading

The purpose of during and just-after reading behaviors is to turn passive readers into active readers. Active readers read metacognitively, monitoring their comprehension and "discussing" ideas with the author.

During reading students should:
- check their understanding of the selection.
- use vocabulary techniques to understand new words.
- relate each paragraph to the selection's main point.

Just after reading students should:
- relate what they read to what they already know.
- adjust information gathered when previewing.

Read actively

To read actively, students should:

- **Think about why they are reading.** A person who is reading for pleasure reads differently from a person who is reading for information. Knowing *why* they are reading is critical to students' success. Students may learn their purpose in reading from their teacher, or they may understand the point of reading from experience in that subject.

- **"Talk back" to the text.** Active readers stop often to ask themselves if they understand what they are reading. They agree or disagree with the author. They also identify the main points and supporting details of their reading.

- **Use text clues.** Remind students that readings often include clues about meaning, such as graphics, photographs, words in bold or italic type, headings, and the like. Headings, for example, signal a new subject or preview what will come next. Subheadings give information about the section.

- **Monitor their comprehension.** Successful readers monitor their understanding of the text. Most students need to be taught to pay attention not just to what they understand, but also to what they do *not* understand. When they are confused, they reread the section, looking for clues. If they're still unclear about meaning, they seek help.

Take notes

All of the strategies in the *Reading Strategies* series require students to take notes after they read. Notes help students retain what they learn. The process of writing important facts and details reinforces their importance and makes them easier to remember.

There are many ways to take notes. Instruction in the *Reading Strategies* series focuses on several of them. Here are some guidelines for helping students take useful notes:

- **Taking good notes depends on selectivity.** Notes should contain only the most important points of the reading.

- **First, write the main points.** The main point may be in one paragraph or several. The process of deciding what a main point is spurs students to become active readers. Ask students what they think is the main point (or points) in a short selection from their textbook.

- **Next, write the supporting details.** The supporting details back up or tell more about the main point. Ask students what information they think supports the main point or points in the selection you chose.

Postreading

The final step for successful reading is reviewing. As with pre- and during-reading activities, postreading activities should become routine. There are many ways to review reading. Some are listed below. What they have in common is that the reader must synthesize the important points in the reading.

> **During postreading students should:**
> - synthesize the information they read.
> - connect what they read to what they already knew.
> - adjust their previewing techniques for use in future readings.
> - form an opinion about what they have read.

Write a summary

This is the best-known strategy for postreading, and one with proven effectiveness. Introduce this skill in stages. When students first write a summary, suggest that they follow these guidelines:

- Review notes on major points and supporting details before summarizing.

- Divide the writing into manageable sections, and then summarize.

- Pay more attention to the content, less to the mechanics of writing.

- Try not to repeat the writer's words, but paraphrase them instead.

Engage in other postreading activities

Postreading activities can be adjusted to the purpose of the reading. Here are some additional suggestions:

- **Create a graphic organizer.** Making a graphic organizer can help students reorganize their notes to show text organization. See the section on graphic organizers in this book on pages T40–T47.

- **Give an oral summary.** To create a useful oral summary, the speaker has to state the key ideas and give examples so that the listener will understand. Consider asking student pairs to practice this technique by reading two different articles and summarizing them for each other.

- **Revisit predictions.** When they preview, students should make predictions about what they will read. After reading, students can think about what they expected when they previewed. How did what they actually learned differ from what they thought they might learn? Stress that predicting improves with practice and that there is no penalty for incorrect predictions. As students learn to analyze clues, their predictions will become more accurate.

- **Solve a problem; create a diagram.** Some readings may lend themselves to a type of review that is different from a summary. For example, a selection in a math textbook may be better reviewed by having students create new problems and then solve them. A process described in a science textbook may be more effectively reviewed by drawing a diagram. Suggest that students vary their reviews to suit each reading.

Reading in Mathematics

In many mathematics texts, word problems and connected text have replaced purely numerical practice exercises. Many students who have been successful with calculation are now challenged by math reading. Students may need new strategies to approach math reading successfully because both conceptual and procedural knowledge is required.

The Demands of Reading in Mathematics

Mathematics textbooks are marked by particular elements—density of numbers and symbols, concepts that build, everyday words that have different meanings in mathematics, words that indicate operations, and equations and symbols.

An often overlooked tool in math textbooks is information in a glossary or other appendix and in tables and diagrams. Remind students to refer to these aids as they read and study.

- **Density of ideas** Because mathematic ideas are presented compactly, math reading requires a slower reading rate than narrative text. Suggest that to master mathematics texts, students should stop when they do not understand an idea, and they should seek an explanation.

- **Mathematics concepts that build** Mathematics understanding builds not only within a selection, but also from selection to selection. Suggest that students backtrack to see if comprehension problems stem from a lack of understanding of the math on which the lesson is based.

- **Equations and symbols** In mathematics reading, equations and symbols serve as words. Help students understand that these devices are often the point of the text. Have students pay close attention to equations and restate them in words or sentences.

- **Relevant details in word problems** Many students do not understand that some details in a word problem will not help them solve the problem. Help students by writing a word problem on the board and crossing out details that are not necessary to find the solution.

Text Structures in Mathematics

When students understand the way a text is organized, they can better predict what will be next and understand the author's point. Students should watch for the common math text patterns.

- **Main idea and details** When students identify this text structure, they can use a wheel-and-spoke diagram to represent major topics and their supporting details. This diagram will help students organize the information they are learning.

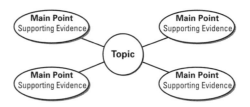

- **Text with diagrams and graphs** In some mathematics texts, the diagram or graph is the main point, and the accompanying text serves as an explanation. Suggest that students keep one finger or pencil eraser on the graph or diagram while they read the explanation.

- **Word problems** Students can deal with word problems by isolating the question and the details needed to answer it. Encourage students to use Poyla's problem-solving sequence: read and understand the problem, devise a plan, carry out the plan, and check that the answer is a reasonable one and that it addresses the problem.

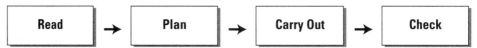

- **Multiple-meaning words** Mathematics words may confuse students who understand the words' non-mathematical meanings. For example, words such as *base, factor, mean, plane, function, interest, principle, domain,* and *relation* have meanings that are specific to math. Help students preview math lessons before they read and record the mathematical meanings of these words.

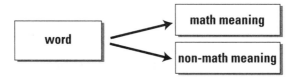

Teaching Tip

You might keep a "math glossary" by the chalkboard so that students can continue to refer to it. Students might copy this list onto the first page of their math notebooks for easy reference. This list could include terms that are specific to math as well as terms that have different meanings in math and in other content areas.

- **Words that indicate operations** Students need to focus on words that indicate operations. Examples of these words and phrases include *divided by, difference, cubed, decrease, halved, increased, less, more than, product, quotient, split equally, sum, squared,* and *remainder*. Ask students what operations these words might indicate. Remind students that the words should signal that the sentence probably describes an operation.

- **Combination of patterns** Students should be alert for a combination of patterns. If students know they will first be reading an equation and then an application of it, they will be better able to grasp the importance of what they are reading. Texts with several patterns can be represented by a variety of graphic organizers.

Teaching the Strategies

Students' success relies on their fully understanding how to apply the strategies with reading selections. In the Unit Lesson Notes, you will see teaching suggestions and think-alouds that you may wish to use to model for students the process of using strategies.

You may choose to teach these lessons to the entire class or to a group. You may also wish to divide the class into four groups and have each group focus on learning one strategy. When the groups feel confident, they might then teach their strategy to the rest of the class.

The graphic organizers in the Student Edition allow students to write a few responses in each step of the strategy. If you prefer to have students go into more depth, you might consider making copies of each strategy's reproducible graphic organizer for every student. These reproducibles are located on pages T40–T47 of this Annotated Teacher's Edition.

Unit 1 Strategy: **PACA**
(pages 6–24)

Teaching Tip

Tell students that when they make predictions, they should think about the *hows* and *whys* of the selection. These questions will help them find the main points of the text.

PACA stands for **P**redicting **A**nd **C**onfirming **A**ctivity. This strategy works well on readings that have topics on which students have some background knowledge. With this information, students can make appropriate predictions. When readers make predictions, they develop an investment in the reading—they want to read to find out if their predictions were accurate.

Introduce the Strategy

Explain what the acronym PACA represents. Then ask students what kind of reading this strategy would be best for. Students may say that it would work best for a topic about which they have some prior knowledge.

Suggest to students that they may have some prior knowledge about a topic even if they do not know a great deal about it. They also can develop prior knowledge about a topic by previewing the reading. In this way, they will get a general sense of the topic so that they will be able to make some predictions.

The Strategy

P = Predicting
A = And
C = Confirming
A = Activity

Model the Strategy

If you are presenting this strategy to the whole class, draw the PACA graphic on the board, make a copy for every student, or make an overhead transparency. You can use the reproducible on page T40 of this Annotated Teacher's Edition for this purpose. Model the strategy with students by adding notes to the PACA chart as you verbalize your thoughts.

Explain what students will write in each section of the PACA graphic. They will write predictions in the Predictions column. They will write checks in the small box in the corner of a prediction that proved to be correct. They will revise predictions that were incorrect, and they will write stars in the small box of those predictions. They will cross out predictions that were incorrect. In the Support column, they will write details that explain each prediction.

Emphasize that there are no penalties for incorrect predictions. Students must develop their ability to use clues to make correct predictions. Also, even experienced readers make incorrect predictions at times, especially if the topic is unfamiliar. Students' aim is to make increasingly accurate predictions by honing their ability to detect clues when previewing.

Because students will probably have some familiarity with the topic of the selection on pages 7–9, you may not need to develop their prior knowledge. If this is not the case, engage students in a discussion about school uniforms. Tell students that in some schools, often in parochial or private schools, students are required to wear uniforms. Some people believe that uniforms could improve public-school students' performance and discipline.

Have students follow along as you model the use of the PACA strategy with the lesson on pages 6–9 of the Student Edition.

Modeling PACA

You may wish to use this or your own think-aloud plan to model using the PACA reading strategy.

Teaching Tip

Emphasize that students should think about the reasons an author gives for any opinions he or she presents. Evaluating opinions will help students learn to support their own predictions with facts.

Think-aloud Lesson Plan

Step 1. *First, I'll think about what I know about school uniforms. I know that students in private schools often wear uniforms and that some parents believe public-school students should wear them, too. I think students should have some voice in this debate. It might be good to wear uniforms because I wouldn't have to decide what to wear every morning, but I'm not sure I want other people telling me what to wear.*

I'll preview the reading to see what it will tell me. I'll look at the title, the subheadings, the photos, the first and last paragraphs, and the topic sentences. I see that this is a debate, so I'll probably read about both sides of the issue. The first paragraph of the section that's against uniforms tells me that the writer thinks that people would probably drop out if they were forced to wear uniforms. The picture shows students getting along and talking about something. They're all dressed differently, and they seem to be pretty happy. Then the writer says that uniforms would cost more and that violence wouldn't stop. She also thinks she has a constitutional right to express herself by dressing as she wants to.

[Continue in this way with the section in favor of school uniforms.]

I see that the student who has begun the PACA chart on page 6 has predicted that the writer who is against uniforms will say they cost more. The writer who is for school uniforms will say uniforms will cost less than regular clothing. My prediction about the debate against uniforms is that the writer will say that students should be allowed to dress as they want because uniforms won't stop violence.

Step 2. *Now, I'll read the debate. As I read, I'll look for my predictions to see if I was right. I'll also look to see why my predictions were right—or wrong. Let's read the article together.*

[Read the article with the class, either aloud or silently.]

Step 3. *I'll look back at the PACA chart to check my predictions. I see that the student has checked both of her predictions in the chart on page 9. Then she's added support for them in the Support column. I predicted that the writer who is against uniforms would say that uniforms won't stop violence, and I was right. I'll make a check in the small box. My support for that prediction is that she says that people will fight whether they're wearing uniforms or not. I'll write that in the Support box.*

Review the Strategy

Ask students to practice this strategy on another reading assignment (or you might want to choose an appropriate selection). Tell students that as they work, they should feel free to ask questions to clarify what they do not understand. This will help them feel comfortable when using the strategy again on their own.

Predictions	Support

How to Use the Strategy

The following graphic demonstrates how the PACA strategy might work for a selection on reproduction without seeds.

Predictions	Support
Stems can reproduce without seeds ✓	Tubers, bulbs, corms are underground stems that reproduce
~~All reproduction without seeds based on stems or roots~~	
Leaves can reproduce *	Some plants produce little plantlets to reproduce

Lesson 1 (pages 10–13)
Number Patterns

Selection Summary
This selection focuses on the patterns numbers can take, both in mathematics and in everyday life. First, the reader learns about the Fibonacci sequence, which is the pattern of numbers formed when 1 is added to 1 and then that number is added to the next number formed, and so on. The article discusses the number patterns in everyday life, such as the sales predictions that a small business can make based on the previous years' sales.

Strategy Notes
You might note to students that, as in other content-area readings, previewing will facilitate their reading in mathematics. You can model that when students preview, they are likely to see that the topic deals with patterns such as projecting sales figures.

Vocabulary Tip
The Vocabulary Tip on page 10 refers to the use of context clues to find the meaning of a new word. Refer students to Exercises 2 and 3 in the Vocabulary Strategies for reinforcement of context clues.

ESL/LEP Notes
As students begin this section on mathematics, encourage them to begin a new section in their vocabulary notebooks for words in English that have to do with this subject. If students separate unknown words in English by subject, they will be able to find those words again more easily when they need to find them in order to understand a definition.

Cooperative Learning
Number patterns can be a fascinating topic. Divide students into groups, and have them look for and analyze the number patterns they see in the world. First, ask students to spend a day collecting these patterns on their own. Then ask groups to come together and discuss the patterns that the members collected. Have groups analyze and categorize the types of patterns they found.

Lesson 2 (pages 14–16)
Russian Peasant Multiplication Method

Selection Summary
In this selection, students learn about the Russian Peasant Multiplication Method, which relies on addition, not multiplication, to find the product of two factors.

To use this method, students continue to halve one number and double the other until the halved number is 1. Then the students circle the even numbers in the halves column, cross out the numbers across from these in the double column, and add the remaining numbers in the double column. This sum is the answer.

Strategy Notes
The impulse of some students facing mathematics writing is to pay *less* attention to the numbers and formulas instead of more. Remind these students that understanding in mathematics depends on mastering these formulas and relationships among numbers.

Tell students that when they come across a series of set-aside numbers in mathematics writing, they need to train themselves to stop and pay closer attention because those numbers often signal that a concept important to understanding the selection is being presented.

ESL/LEP Notes
One encouraging fact about mathematics writing for English language learners is that numbers are, for the most part, the information that matters. Students learning English should understand that if they are able to first identify and then decipher the formulas in a mathematics piece, they can often understand the rest more easily.

Extension
Students can work in pairs to try using the Russian Peasant Method. Have students take turns creating multiplication problems to be solved using this method, and see how easily they can use it. You might want to suggest that students also try having one member of the pair multiply in the traditional way and the other use the Russian Peasant way. Which is faster?

Lesson 3 (pages 17–19)
Finding Relevant Information

Selection Summary

This selection focuses on a central problem with solving word problems—separating relevant from irrelevant information. The selection suggests that students follow these steps when faced with word problems: (1) read the problem carefully to decide what is being asked, (2) make a list of information contained in the problem, (3) look over the list and cross off irrelevant information, and (4) use the relevant information to solve the problem.

The selection then discusses how to use this method on a sample word problem dealing with discovering the November total for a store's sales.

Strategy Notes

When students make predictions about selections that have mathematical information, they need to remember to focus on the *math* that the selection is teaching.

When they preview, students should think about what appears to be the point of the selection—usually, this will be a mathematically based formula or concept. They should then pay less attention to the additional material in the selection. When students can separate essential from nonessential information, they will be better able to figure out the mathematical point of a problem.

Vocabulary Tip

The Vocabulary Tip on page 17 refers to the use of context clues to find the meaning of a new word. Refer students to Exercises 2 and 3 in the Vocabulary Strategies for reinforcement of context clues.

ESL/LEP Notes

Encourage English language learners to write unfamiliar expressions and idioms when they are reading. If the unfamiliar words are an impediment to their understanding of the selection, tell students to check with a native English speaker to explain the term or idiom.

If the unknown term does not halt the flow of understanding, suggest students write the words and ask a native English speaker to explain them later. However, students should not proceed with their reading if the word they do not understand is a term. Stress to students that all terms must be understood so that the student will be able to comprehend the meaning of the mathematical concept.

Extension

Word problems are a part of most mathematics instruction. Make sure students understand the point of this selection by asking them to solve several word problems using this technique. You may want to ask a volunteer to use a sample problem from a math textbook and go through the technique step-by-step for the class, if necessary.

In addition, you might have students take turns explaining to other students or to a younger child the way they solved problems. Or consider having them write a paragraph in which they explain their method for solving the problem.

Lesson 4 (pages 20–22)
Guess and Check

Selection Summary

Solving many kinds of word problems depends on making good guesses. There is a strategy to doing this. Step 1 is identifying what you need to find out. Step 2 is identifying what you already know. Step 3 is using this knowledge to make a guess. Students then check their guesses to see if they make sense. If necessary, students repeat the process until they come up with a reasonable guess. Each of these steps leads the solver closer to a solution.

Strategy Notes

Although this article is about math, it focuses on a process, not a formula. Students should be able to understand this if they preview. Previewing will enable students to make predictions that focus on what they are reading, not necessarily on what they might expect to read. Good predictions in reading are not based on random guesses but on information gained from previewing. Student predictions gradually should show an understanding of the process of predicting. Also, their predictions should become increasingly accurate.

Vocabulary Tip

The Vocabulary Tip on page 20 refers to the use of context clues to find the meaning of a new word. Refer students to Exercises 2 and 3 in the Vocabulary Strategies for reinforcement of context clues.

ESL/LEP Notes

English language learners can sometimes benefit from using pictures or illustrations to remind them of important facts in reading. Their notes, for example, may contain small pictures that remind them of the important facts. Those pictures reinforce understanding of the English words that the student should also be writing.

Extension

Students can work in groups to find or create problems that can be solved using the guess-and-check method. When groups have several problems, have them put all the problems into a hat. Each group can draw a problem and show how to use the guess-and-check method to solve it. Each group might then present to the class the problem and the process it used to solve the problem.

Unit 2 Strategy: **DRTA**
(pages 25–44)

Teaching Tip

Point out to students that they'll understand their reading better if they think about the topic before they read. This involves thinking about what they know and looking for text clues about what they will read.

This strategy—Directed Reading and Thinking Activity—is based on the ability of students to make valid predictions about what they will read. DRTA works best with topics that students have some familiarity with, although students can acquire familiarity with a topic by previewing carefully. Previewing requires students to look quickly at text and form some ideas about content. Inexperienced readers often have difficulty with comprehension because they have not thought about what they will read. Previewing helps students think about a reading in a systematic way.

Introduce the Strategy

Explain that DRTA stands for Directed Reading and Thinking Activity. This strategy requires a three-step process of making predictions, reading actively, and reviewing what was read. Tell students that when they know even a little about a topic, the DRTA strategy will help them access this knowledge and use it as they read.

The Strategy

D = Directed
R = Reading and
T = Thinking
A = Activity

Students' first step is to preview the reading, paying close attention to the title, subheadings, first and last paragraphs, and any photos or illustrations they see. Tell students to use this information to determine the topic and to predict some main points that the author will make. Students should also think about what they already know about the topic. They should write this information in the Preview box of their DRTA chart. As they read, they should think about what they wrote.

The next step is to read the selection and then take notes about what they learned. Students' notes should reflect on their predictions and include the main points of the selection. If a prediction was wrong, tell students to cross it out to avoid confusion later.

Finally, ask students to review what they have learned in the Review box. In many cases, students will write a summary as a review. Remind students that to write a summary, they must include the main points of the article. For some selections, they might review in another way that makes sense, such as working out a math problem to demonstrate the understanding of a new concept. In any case, reviewing will help students make sure they understand—and remember—what is important in what they read.

Teaching Tip

Graphics often summarize the issues the selection presents. Be sure students understand how to read and interpret the sports graphics on pages 26 and 27. You might also have students redraw them.

Model the Strategy

If you are presenting this strategy to the whole class, draw a DRTA chart on the board, make a copy for every student, or make an overhead transparency. You can use the reproducible on page T41 of this Annotated Teacher's Edition for this purpose. Model the strategy with students by adding notes to the chart as you verbalize your thoughts.

As you model this strategy, point out the thoughts of the student who is using DRTA to understand the selection. These appear in italic type on page 25 of the Student Edition. Also work with students to understand the sports graphics on pages 26 and 27. These charts encapsulate the author's ideas about the topic.

Have students follow along as you model the use of the DRTA strategy with the lesson on pages 25–28 of the Student Edition. **Think-aloud Lesson Plan**

Modeling DRTA

You may wish to use this or your own think-aloud plan to model using the outlining reading strategy.

Step 1. *First, I'll preview the selection. The title and the subheadings tell me I'll read about the chances of becoming a pro basketball or football player. I know it's hard to become a pro, and it looks like the graphics on pages 26 and 27 show me how hard it is. The chances are even smaller than I thought. It seems that the student had the same thought. He wrote in the DRTA chart on page 26 that in basketball, only 2.6 percent of high-school players will go pro out of 156,000 total players. That's a pretty low number.*

The first and last paragraphs and the topic sentences tell me that the rest of the article explains these numbers. I'll add a prediction to the student's chart about the chances of going pro in football. It looks as if only a few more football players make the pros. Out of 274,000 high-school seniors playing football, only 0.5 percent go pro.

Step 2. *Now, I'll read to check my ideas and look for details about these formulas. Let's read the article together.*

[Read the article with the class, either aloud or silently.]

Now I'll look at my predictions. I was right that only 0.5 percent of high-school football players go pro. The article explains each step from high school through college. That means even though Johnny Jackson, on my school's team, is a great player, he's right that he needs to do his homework before he goes out to the field to practice.

Step 3. *I'll use my DRTA chart to summarize the article. I see the student began by saying that the chances of making a pro team aren't good. I'll continue by explaining the chances of going pro in basketball and in football. I'll use the graphics on pages 26 and 27 to check my figures.*

Review the Strategy

Ask students to practice this strategy on another reading assignment (or you might want to choose an appropriate selection). It would be particularly helpful for students to practice previewing. This is a skill they can use with all types of informational reading. It can help them form a scaffold for their learning by preparing them for what they will read.

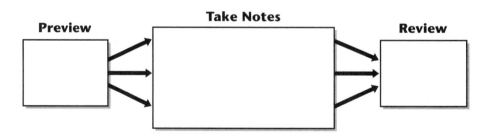

Preview   **Take Notes**   **Review**

How to Use the Strategy

The following graphic demonstrates how the DRTA strategy might work for a science selection on vertebrates.

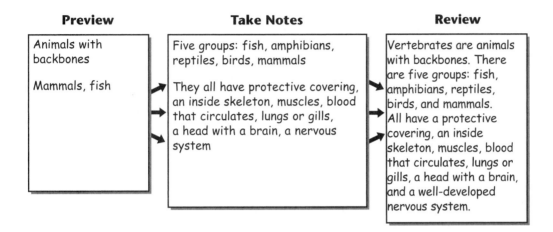

Preview	Take Notes	Review
Animals with backbones Mammals, fish	Five groups: fish, amphibians, reptiles, birds, mammals They all have protective covering, an inside skeleton, muscles, blood that circulates, lungs or gills, a head with a brain, a nervous system	Vertebrates are animals with backbones. There are five groups: fish, amphibians, reptiles, birds, and mammals. All have a protective covering, an inside skeleton, muscles, blood that circulates, lungs or gills, a head with a brain, and a well-developed nervous system.

Lesson 5 (pages 29–31)
The Million-Dollar Minute

Selection Summary

This selection focuses on the amount of money sponsors pay television networks for air time for their commercials. Advertisers are willing to spend plenty because Americans spend, on average, 7 to 8 hours per day in front of the TV set.

In the United States, 13 minutes per hour are devoted to commercials; in Japan and France, the total is less than 1 minute per hour.

The amount charged for air time depends on the size of the audience. The fees are set by "cost per thousand TV viewers," or CPM. For example, for a show with a CPM of $30 per minute and an audience of 1 million, a one-minute commercial would cost $30,000.

A hit show can command premium rates. Advertisements for 30 seconds in the Super Bowl, for example, may cost as much as $1 million. On the other hand, a program with low ratings in Washington State recently cost an advertiser only $3,780 for a minute.

Strategy Notes

Focus on the process of making predictions using the DRTA chart. Good predictions in reading are based not on random guesses, but on information gained from previewing. Reinforce that when students preview, they are looking for main ideas in titles, formulas, summary and introductory paragraphs, topic sentences, photos, illustrations, and so on. Student predictions in this article should focus on determining the price of TV advertising time.

ESL/LEP Notes

Students learning English can sometimes benefit from drawing pictures or illustrations to help them understand and remember important facts. These can serve as a kind of illustrated dictionary. Students may wish to write a description of the drawings they make in both English and their native language.

Cooperative Learning

Students can work in groups to simulate buying advertising time on a network. Within the group, some students can be buyers of time and establish both a budget and a set of clients; others can be sellers with shows that have different simulated ratings and prices. Students can come together to buy and sell television time.

Lesson 6 (pages 32–34)
Playing the Market

Selection Summary

The stock market was invented in the United States when colonial banks began selling shares of their businesses during the Revolutionary War to raise money for the fight against Great Britain. After the war, those agreements to own shares were the beginning of the New York Stock Exchange in New York City.

The stock market is open to anyone, but a buyer and a seller are required. The buyer contacts a broker, who buys stock for him or her. The buyer also pays the broker a commission. The price of a company's shares rises and falls. If the value of a stock goes up, the stock is worth more than when the buyer bought it. If the value of a stock goes down, the stock is worth less than when the buyer bought it.

The value of stocks is constantly changing. Today, billions of dollars worth of stock changes hands at the New York Stock Exchange.

Strategy Notes
Most students will have heard of the stock market, even if their families don't own stock. Ask students to think about what they already know about the stock market before they begin previewing. Their predictions should be a combination of what they already know and what they learn from previewing.

Remind students to cross out predictions that prove wrong. If they don't cross out wrong predictions, students may find themselves confused about what is really in the article.

Also emphasize that there is no penalty for incorrect predictions. Students will find that their predictions will become more accurate over time, as they learn how to preview. They will more easily read the clues an author gives about what will be in the selection, so their predictions will more closely reflect the information that is actually presented in the reading.

Vocabulary Tip
The Vocabulary Tip on page 32 refers to the use of context clues to find the meaning of a new word. Refer students to Exercises 2 and 3 in the Vocabulary Strategies for reinforcement of context clues.

ESL/LEP Notes
Some of the terms in this article may confuse English-language learners because they have little knowledge of the stock market. Ask students to make a list of unfamiliar terms. Then have them ask for help from other students in order to understand these terms.

Extension
Every week day there is information in the newspaper about how the stock market has performed. Ask students to collect these reports for a week and then write a summary of the stock market's activity for that week. You might ask them to choose one stock to track for the week.

Lesson 7 (pages 35–37)
Nielsen Ratings

Selection Summary
Television is a medium for advertisers as well as viewers. Advertisers choose shows during which to advertise their products based on the audience they wish to reach. One way advertisers decide if their commercials are running on the right shows is to rely on the Nielsen ratings.

Nielsen Media Research produces these ratings; it uses meters to track viewership of random TV watchers. The profile of the television watcher is registered, along with the show he or she is watching. This information makes up the ratings. Each night, the company collects the information on what was watched that day. The next day, the information is sent out to networks and advertisers. That information helps advertisers decide what shows to spend advertising money on and helps programmers set advertising rates.

Strategy Notes
This mathematics reading has the numbers and mathematical information embedded in a narrative. When students face this kind of mathematics writing, it is important for them to unearth the math from the narrative. Suggest that when students take their notes for a piece such as this, they make sure that those notes contain the mathematical information that is important. Tell students to include the formulas that they find when they preview in the Preview boxes of their DRTA charts.

Vocabulary Tip

The Vocabulary Tips on pages 35 and 36 refer to the use of related words and context clues to find the meaning of a new word. Refer students to Exercises 2, 3, and 4 for reinforcement of context clues and using related words.

ESL/LEP Notes

In order to demonstrate their understanding of the terms, ask students to write out the equations that appear in this selection by using phrases or by drawing pictures.

Extension

Ask students to watch an hour-long television program and, noting the show, to take notes about what commercials are shown. Have students analyze the commercials. What audience is the advertiser trying to reach? Why did you reach this conclusion? Students can write a report that explains what they learned and why they came to the conclusion they did.

Internet Connection

http://www.nielsenmedia.com/
NielsenMedia.com explains what Nielsen ratings are, how they work, and what they really mean. By clicking on the Ratings 101 link, students can view a graphic representation of the formulas used to calculate HUT (Households Using TV), Rating, and Share.

Lesson 8 (pages 39–42)
Mental Math

Selection Summary

The selection suggests that students can calculate mathematical problems in their heads and it explains how mental math works using three different methods: working with round numbers, adding by place value, and multiplying the pieces. The article introduces each of these methods using a step-by-step approach that breaks down each method for the student. Tell students that they can use mental math both in the classroom and during the course of daily living.

Strategy Notes

When students make predictions about selections that are concerned with mathematical information, they need to remember to focus on the *math* in the selection. When they are previewing, students should think about what appears to be the point of the selection—usually, this will be a mathematically based formula or concept—and pay less attention to the supporting material. When students have a good idea of the mathematical point, they will be better able to make sense of the supporting information.

ESL/LEP Notes

Make sure students understand the math steps in each method completely before they turn to the next step. English language learners who move to the next step before completely understanding the one they are on risk becoming confused. Ask students to write the steps for each method in their own words and to make sure they understand the step before moving to the next one.

Extension

Mental math is a skill that students can use extensively in their daily lives. Make sure students understand the point of this selection by asking them to solve several problems using the methods. You may want to ask a volunteer to use a sample problem and go through the technique step-by-step for the class, if necessary.

Unit 3 Strategy: KWL PLUS

(pages 45–64)

Teaching Tip

Before you begin this lesson, review page 1 of the Student Edition with students. This page discusses how to ask questions with informational text.

This reading strategy was developed by Ogle (1986) and is now in wide use. It helps students access their knowledge on a topic so they can add the new information to what they already know. KWL Plus works particularly well for selections about which a reader has some background knowledge.

Introduce the Strategy

Explain that KWL stands for "Know," "Want to Know," and "Learned." Tell students that this reading strategy was designed with three important parts. Readers first think about what they will read, which helps them connect what they already know to what they will learn. This information goes in the K column of their KWL charts. Their next step is to write questions about what they want to learn in the W column of their charts. Then students read the selection. After they read, students take notes on what they have learned in the L section of their charts. The notes should help students find answers to the questions they have asked and determine the major ideas in the reading. The "Plus" involves writing a summary so that students will remember what they have read.

The Strategy

K = What I know
W = What I want to
    know
L = What I've learned
Plus = a summary of
       the reading

If students have no prior knowledge of a topic, help them develop a scaffold for learning. To do this, you may wish to display photographs or show a video that relates to the topic. If none is available, provide students with some background information. Students might also benefit from a brainstorming session in which they discuss as a class what they know about the topic.

Model the Strategy

If you are presenting this strategy to the whole class, draw the KWL graphic on the board, make a copy for every student, or make an overhead transparency. You can use the reproducible on page T42 of this Annotated Teacher's Edition for this purpose. Model the strategy with students by making notes on the KWL chart as you verbalize your thoughts.

When students use the KWL strategy, they create questions about what they would like to learn from the reading. Asking questions is a particularly difficult skill. Students often ask questions about minor details that do not help them discover the major ideas in the reading. Encourage students to develop their questioning skills by having them focus on *why* and *how* questions. These questions can help students understand the meaning of the entire selection.

Have students follow along as you model the use of the KWL strategy with the lesson on pages 45–48 of the Student Edition.

**Modeling KWL
Plus**

You may wish to use
this or your own
think-aloud plan to
model using the KWL
Plus reading strategy.

Teaching Tip

Model asking
questions by turning
topic sentences into
questions such as,
"Why is it easy to find
people who get
excited about the
money that pro
athletes make?"

Think-aloud Lesson Plan

Step 1. *What do I know about the topic? I'll preview the article so I know what it's about. The title on page 46 and the photograph on page 47 tell me that the article is about pro athletes' salaries. The title also tells me that this is a debate, so I'll probably read about both sides of the issue.*

I don't know much about pro athletes' salaries, so I'll preview a little more. I'll read the first and last paragraphs and the first sentence of each paragraph. I see that the first paragraph tells me that the writer thinks that players make too much money. The last paragraph talks about how players who make a lot of money just make the system work for them. Now, I'll make notes about these things in the K column of my KWL chart.

Step 2. *Now, I'll make up some questions about what I want to know about pro athletes' salaries. I want to know what the arguments are against high salaries. I see that the student asked about the arguments against high salaries, too. I also see that the student asked for arguments for high salaries in the chart on page 46. I think I'll add that question to the W section of my chart.*

Step 3. *My next step is to read the article carefully. I'll think about what I know as I read and look for answers to the questions I wrote. Let's read the article together.*

[Read the article with the class, either aloud or silently.]

Now, I'll take notes about what I learned from the reading. I'll also try to answer the questions I wrote in the W section of my KWL chart. The answer to my question about arguments against high salaries seems to be that pro athletes don't deserve them. They don't do anything to help the world. The writer also says that they are too pampered and think that they are better than "ordinary" people.

Step 4. *My last step is to summarize what I've learned so I'll remember it. What are the main points of the article? I learned that there are two sides to this debate. I'll add some details about the arguments for and against high salaries for pro athletes. The argument against high salaries is that the pro athletes don't do anything to help the world. The argument for high salaries is that they make money for their employers.*

Review the Strategy

Tell students that this way of reading—thinking about what they know, reading the selection, taking notes about it, and then reviewing by writing a summary—will improve their ability to both understand and remember what they read. Explain also that the notes they take using this strategy will help them review for tests on the subject.

K (What I know)	W (What I want to know)	L (What I've learned)

How to Use the Strategy

The following graphic demonstrates how the KWL Plus strategy might work for a selection on the life of pioneers in the U.S. West.

K (What I know)	W (What I want to know)	L (What I've learned)
Pioneers had hard lives Had to grow own food Lived far from towns	What was daily life like? Did all pioneers live in log houses?	Everyone worked hard: men plowed fields; women gardened, cooked, cleaned, and plowed; children did farm and home chores. Houses: dugouts, sod or earth homes, log cabins where trees were common.

Lesson 9 (pages 49–52)
Average Achievement

Selection Summary

This selection focuses on the ways that people use averages. Averages give information about overall performance, from bowling averages to average number of hours worked per week.

People also calculate averages to determine rank. For example, baseball averages include batting averages, which are determined by dividing the number of hits a player gets by the number of times he bats. In 1995, for example, Albert Belle's batting average was .317. In 1998, he improved his average to .328 and averaged more hits that year. Although Mark McGwire broke the record for most single-season home runs, his batting average was only .299. Home runs and singles are the same when determining batting average.

Strategy Notes

You might show students that in mathematics reading, previewing may reveal that the subject is more accessible than the students had thought. You can model that when a student previews, he or she is likely to see that the topic deals with averages he or she is familiar with, such as batting averages.

Vocabulary Tip

The Vocabulary Tip on page 49 refers to the use of related words to find the meaning of a new word. Refer students to Exercise 4 for reinforcement of using related words.

ESL/LEP Notes

As students begin this section on mathematics, encourage them to make a new section in their vocabulary notebooks for words in English that have to do with this subject. If they separate new words in English by subject, students will be more easily able to find those words again to help them understand a definition.

Extension

Ask students to choose any subject that is amenable to averaging and work out the averages. Examples might range from test grades to times a student drinks milk with lunch. Students can share their averages with the class.

Lesson 10 (pages 53–55)
Donna Auguste, American Dreamer

Selection Summary

The focus of this selection is a woman who invented the Newton, a notebook computer. As a child, Donna Auguste was interested in math and science. In seventh grade, she discovered computers and became enchanted with them.

She began saving money for college and won a scholarship to the University of California at Berkeley. At college, she ran into plenty of male students who did not want to work with a woman. She shrugged that off and got her undergraduate degree in electrical engineering and computer science and her graduate degree at Carnegie Mellon University.

In her first job, she specialized in artificial intelligence. Then Auguste joined Apple, where she led the team designing the Newton. Today, she heads her own company that develops computer technologies.

Strategy Notes

This article focuses on mathematics as it relates to life. Point out that in this selection, the focus is not on computation but on how math and life connect. Math itself is less important. When students preview, they need to determine the point of the reading so they can get the most out of it.

Vocabulary Tip

The Vocabulary Tips on pages 54 and 55 refer to the use of context clues and related words to find the meaning of a new word. Refer students to Exercises 2, 3, and 4 for reinforcement of context clues and using related words.

ESL/LEP Notes

After students have finished their KWL charts, ask them to show their charts to you and to explain how they went about their work. Suggest that students give you a step-by-step analysis of how they did the steps of the strategy and the reading. Students' analyses should give you a good idea of their ability to understand and use this strategy.

Extension

Students can look in a newspaper's technology section and report on the latest research in computer technology. What might we expect in the future? Ask students to find a relevant article, write a summary of it, and share the summary with the class.

Lesson 11 (pages 57–59)
Balancing a Checking Account

Selection Summary

This selection explains the process of balancing a checkbook. First, account holders make a

deposit, which they list in their record books, as well as the date the deposit was made. Next, account holders write checks on the money in the account, recording the check numbers, amount, the person each check was written to, and the dates.

At the end of the month, the bank sends a statement that lists all deposits and checks on the account. To balance the account, account holders first deduct any bank fees from the total or add any interest. Then they compare canceled checks with the amounts recorded in the record book. They put check marks next to checks the bank has paid.

Strategy Notes

This selection is essentially a narrative that could be broken into steps. Suggest that as students take notes for mathematics selections such as this, they write their notes as a series of numbered steps. You could also ask one student to take notes in narrative form and another to take notes as a series of steps; then have the students compare their notes. Which is easier to review and understand?

Suggest that students use these notes to help them complete their KWL charts. Remind students to record what they know about balancing a checking account in the K column, what they want to know in the W column, and what they learn in the L column.

Vocabulary Tip

The Vocabulary Tip on page 57 refers to the use of context clues to find the meaning of a new word. Refer students to Exercises 2 and 3 for reinforcement of context clues.

ESL/LEP Notes

In mathematics reading, as in science reading, it is easy for English language learners to get lost unless they understand each step before they proceed to the next step. Caution students to ask for help, if necessary, as they read.

Extension

Have students create mock checking accounts, deposits, and checks to practice the skill of keeping and balancing a checkbook. When students have written 10 "checks," ask them to balance their checkbooks. Have students trade information with another student and see if they can balance each others' checkbooks.

Internet Connection
http://www.nationalbankofalaska.com/bankingb.htm
Banking Basics for Elementary Kids provides students with banking basics as well as definitions of related banking terms, which include *balance*, *income*, *interest*, and *withdrawal*.

Lesson 12 (pages 60–62)
Paying Taxes

Selection Summary
This selection considers the subject of taxes. It discusses the uses to which taxes are put, which include schools, roads, and the police and fire departments. The article details the types of taxes people pay, from sales tax to income tax.

The author discusses how state income taxes are usually calculated at a proportional rate—the rate stays the same regardless of how much you make. Federal income tax is progressive—the rate depends on how much a person earns, meaning that the more you make, the higher the tax is. Federal tax money is paid to the Internal Revenue Service, which collects taxes.

Strategy Notes
You might consider using this selection as a demonstration of the usefulness of strategies. Divide the class in half. Have one half use the KWL Plus strategy to answer the questions, and have the other half simply read the selection and then answer the questions.

After students have completed the lesson, discuss the difference that using a strategy made to students' understanding. Students might want to discuss what they were thinking as they used, or did not use, the strategy.

Vocabulary Tip
The Vocabulary Tip on page 60 refers to the use of context clues to find the meaning of a new word. Refer students to Exercises 2 and 3 for reinforcement of context clues.

ESL/LEP Notes
Ask English-language learners to pair up with native English speakers. Ask the students to show their understanding of the terms by calculating proportional tax and progressive tax.

Curriculum Connections: Social Studies
Students can do some research to find out the state, city, and county taxes people pay where they live and what services these taxes buy. Students can turn that information into a bar or circle graph that shows where the money goes for each kind of tax. Then they can compare the uses to which tax money is put.

Unit 4 Strategy: Concept Building
(pages 65–84)

Teaching Tip

Point out to students that understanding the basic concepts will make the harder concepts easier to understand.

This strategy works best for writing that defines and expands on one topic. It can work particularly well for math and science selections, in which understanding concepts is crucial to understanding the next topic. It can also work well in other context areas when the task is to fully understand a basic term so that a foundation of knowledge can be built.

Introduce the Strategy
Explain to students that a concept is an idea or general term. Tell them that the Concept Building strategy is useful whenever reading centers on explaining one topic because it asks them not only to define the term but also to give examples or explain the process discussed. Tell students that this strategy is useful for areas of knowledge that require a foundation of basic terms.

The Strategy

Step 1: Concept
Step 2: Definition or Formula
Step 3: Evidence or Steps
Step 4: Review or Examples

Explain what students will write in each section of the Concept Building chart. They will look for clues to identify the concept by previewing to find words in bold type, in a numbered list, in a box, and in illustrations. They will define the concept in the Definition or Formula box. They will write the evidence or details that explain the concept in the Evidence or Steps box. In the Review or Examples box, they will summarize the concept or work out math problems they create to demonstrate understanding.

Model the Strategy
If you are presenting this strategy to the whole class, draw the Concept Building graphic on the board, make a copy for every student, or make an overhead transparency. You can use the reproducible on page T43 of this Annotated Teacher's Edition for this purpose. Model this strategy with students by making notes on the Concept Building graphic as you verbalize your thoughts.

Point out the different parts of the Concept Building diagram on the transparency or on the board. Explain that students should pay attention to visual clues that signal an important concept or formula. Tell students that the strategy will help them build their knowledge about a more complex topic by assuring them that they understand the more elementary topic.

Have students follow along as you model the use of the Concept Building strategy with the lessons on pages 65–68 of the Student Edition.

Modeling Concept Building

You may wish to use this or your own think-aloud plan to model the Concept Building strategy.

Think-aloud Lesson Plan
Step 1. *I'll preview the article to find the main concept. The title tells me that this article is probably about sleep. I'll look for signals in the article such as bold type, lists, and illustrations. NREM and REM are in bold type, so these are probably the main concepts. I'll write NREM and REM in the Concept column. On page 65, I see the student made the same choice. She wrote "NREM" and "REM" in the Concept boxes.*

I see a list of stages in bold type. I'm going to preview this list. The stages in this list seem to be describing what happens to people when they sleep. I'm going to guess that this article is about how sleep works.

Point out that an
equation or important
concept will often be
in bold type or in
some other way set
apart from the rest of
the page.

Step 2. *I need to explain the concepts NREM and REM. I know that important concepts in bold type are often followed by a definition. I'll read the sentences in which REM and NREM appear to find definitions for both of these words. Then I'll write both definitions in the Definition or Formula box.*

Step 3. *Now, I'll read the article to learn more about how sleep works. As I read, I'll look for details that explain each concept. Let's read the article together.*

[Read the article with the class, either aloud or silently.]

Now, I'll write the details that I found that explain each concept in the Evidence or Steps box. I'll write, "lasts 5 to 15 minutes" and "sleeper's eyes twitch" for REM. I will also list the four stages of NREM. On page 67, I see that the student made the same choices.

Step 4. *I've completed my chart by filling in all the boxes. Now, I'll review what I learned. I've learned that in REM sleep, the sleeper's eyes move quickly. I learned that first a person goes through 4 stages of NREM sleep. I learned that a person goes from NREM sleep to REM sleep. I also learned that REM sleep can last from 5 to 15 minutes.*

Review the Strategy

Ask students if they have any questions about the strategy. To reinforce this strategy, you might suggest that they find an assignment they feel would be best understood using Concept Building and use it in support of the reading. When students have finished, have a discussion about how and why the strategy worked.

Concept	Definition or Formula	Evidence or Steps	Review or Examples

How To Use the Strategy

The following graphic demonstrates how the Concept Building strategy might work for a math selection on the commutative property of multiplication.

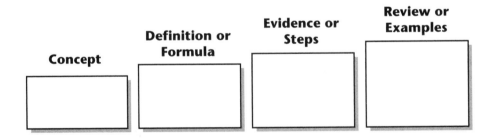

Concept	Definition or Formula	Evidence or Steps	Review or Examples
Commutative property of multiplication	The product of two or more numbers will always be the same, no matter in which order you multiply them.	1. Change the order of numbers you are multiplying. 2. Notice the answer is still the same.	3 X 7 = 21; 7 X 3 = 21 ⎯⎯⎯ 153 X 11 = 1,683; 11 X 153 = 1,683

Lesson 13 (pages 69–71)
Understanding Remainders

Selection Summary

In this selection, students learn more about the relationship of the remainder in a division problem to the practical solution of the problem. The article uses real-life problems as demonstrations.

In one case, a worker has a supply of wire and uses a certain amount to make each birdhouse. He ignores the remaining wire—the remainder—because the extra wire does him no good. In another case, a woman buying lace needs a certain number of yards plus a remainder but must take the remainder into account and buy a larger amount of lace because lace is only sold by the yard. In still another case, a band director who understands remainders orders enough buses to seat all of the band members.

Strategy Notes

This selection is a good choice for Concept Building since it focuses on one specific topic. Model how this article would work for the Concept Building strategy. Draw a large version of the graphic on the board, and ask volunteers to fill out the graphic as the class follows the steps as a group.

ESL/LEP Notes

To gauge student understanding, ask students to use the strategy to read the selection and then explain to you the importance of the remainders in the stories of the worker buying wire and the worker buying lace. If students can explain why the remainder is ignored in the first case and taken into account in the second, they understand the selection.

Extension

Ask students to work with remainders by making a list of real-life situations in which remainders are important and in which they are not. When students finish, they can share their work with classmates to make a class list that illustrates when it is useful to ignore a remainder and when a person must take the remainder into account.

Lesson 14 (pages 72–75)
Reading a Map Scale

Selection Summary

Maps can show many different kinds of information. Maps drawn to scale show the distance between places in a representational, not actual, way. Map scales are usually at the bottom of a map. To use a map scale, students write a proportion and then solve it. Because not every scale is the same, encourage students to analyze every map scale they find to see what it represents.

Strategy Notes

The set-aside formula in this selection, plus the clear single concept, make the Concept Building strategy a good one to use here. Ask students if they understand why the book suggests using the Concept Building strategy with this piece. If students can tell you, they are showing that they can distinguish between the strategies and choose appropriate ones to use with different kinds of reading.

Vocabulary Tip

The Vocabulary Tip on page 72 refers to the use of context clues to find the meaning of a new word. Refer students to Exercises 2 and 3 for reinforcement of context clues.

ESL/LEP Notes

Retelling is a good way to gauge English language learners' understanding. Ask students to use the strategy to read the selection and then explain to you how to use the scale on a map. Then have them explain the equation in the selection and its importance. If students have difficulty, you may need to go back to the strategy lesson to show them how to use the Concept Building strategy with this lesson.

Extension

Bring in maps, and ask students to work in pairs to practice using a variety of map scales. One student can choose a line between two points; the other student can determine the mileage using the scale. Have students check each others' work.

Internet Connection

http://www.csuchico.edu/lbib/maps/
mapscales.html
This site provides an explanation of map scales
accompanied by a short list of examples of
map scales.

Lesson 15 (pages 76–79)
Sample a Survey

Selection Summary

To take a survey, a surveyor asks people what
they think about a topic and then analyzes the
information. The first step is deciding on a topic,
which includes why the information is being
collected. Step 2 is identifying the sample, or the
small group that represents the opinions of a
larger group. Step 3 is deciding on a survey
method, which can be done either by mail, by
telephone, or in person. Step 4 is writing the
questions, which must be clear, focus on the
topic, and not influence the result. Step 5 is
asking the questions. Step 6 is analyzing the data
by first counting it and then understanding
what it means.

Strategy Notes

In a selection like this, the steps are neatly
outlined. Emphasize again to students that when
they see a series of steps that are set in bold type,
they need to make sure that they understand
each step of the process before they move to the
next one.

In the Concept Building strategy, students
should have a firm understanding of the concept
before moving on to the remaining columns of
the chart. If students are having trouble
understanding the Concept Building strategy,
use this lesson to model as a think-aloud. It
provides a clear and simple focus for using the
strategy.

Vocabulary Tip

The Vocabulary Tip on page 77 refers to the use of
prefixes and suffixes to find the meaning of a new
word. Refer students to Exercise 6 for
reinforcement of prefixes and suffixes.

ESL/LEP Notes

Consider modeling how a student struggling with
English should read a narrative mathematics
selection such as this one. Talk as you follow the
text, telling the student what an active reader is
thinking: *In this reading, I'm going to be looking for
the steps and paying attention to each one so I make
sure I understand it before I move on. The first step is
about deciding on a topic. Then I need to think about
why I am collecting information.*

Ask volunteers to model what they are thinking
in the next steps to assess if each student
understands how to identify and understand the
important facts in a mathematics narrative.

Curriculum Connections: Social Studies

The history of public opinion surveys in politics
is worth exploring. For example, you might want
to assign a student to find out more about the
election in which Thomas Dewey was announced
as the winner (because of polls) although Harry
Truman actually won.

Lesson 16 (pages 80–82)
Finding Unit Rate

Selection Summary

Smart shoppers know how to find the unit price
at a grocery store. That is, they can use math to
find the unit price of an item and then compare
items to see which is the better deal.

To determine unit rate, shoppers need to set up
a ratio. For example, with cereal, the shopper
would divide the price of the cereal by the
number of ounces the box contains. With that
unit rate, a shopper could compare that brand
of cereal to another brand. He or she could also
analyze which size box is a better value.

Unit price can also be important in other
situations, such as determining gas mileage,
or the distance a car travels on a tank of gas.
By dividing the number of miles driven by the
amount of gas, consumers can find out their
gas mileage.

Unit rate can show the production rate of a
machine and can be used to make predictions
about how much food and drink a group of
people might need.

Strategy Notes

Stress to students that understanding in mathematics depends on mastering formulas and the relationships among numbers. Tell students that when they come across a formula or a set of steps in mathematics writing, they need to train themselves to stop and pay close attention. Those numbers often signal that a concept important to understanding the selection is being presented.

In the Concept Building strategy, they would write the formula in the Definition or Formula box of their chart. They then would work the formula out in the Evidence or Steps box. Finally, they would review their understanding by working out a new problem using this formula.

Vocabulary Tip

The Vocabulary Tip on page 80 refers to the use of prefixes and suffixes to find the meaning of a new word. Refer students to Exercise 6 for reinforcement of prefixes and suffixes.

ESL/LEP Notes

Tell English language learners that if they are able to first identify and then decipher the formulas in a mathematics reading, they can often understand the rest of the selection. They can also write their notes about the formula or calculation both in their native language and in English.

Extension

Students might accompany the adult members of their families to the grocery store and find the unit price of three competing brands of different types of foods. Students may want to choose different foods ahead of time to look for at the store. At school, students can report on what brands of the food they compared and which ones they found to be the best values.

Internet Connection

http://www.nhptv.org/kn/vs/mathla6.sht
The NHPTV Knowledge Network features math games, puzzles, and problems. It addresses how and why to solve word problems, and it contains printable worksheets.

Vocabulary Strategies Notes

The Student Edition of the *Reading Strategies* series includes vocabulary exercises to help students learn how to understand the meaning of unknown words. When students are puzzled by important words, comprehension is halted. Often, students stop reading. The exercises in the Vocabulary Strategies offer students methods to understand new words.

Using the Vocabulary Exercises

You may want to use these exercises to help students increase their reading comprehension skills or to diagnose reading difficulties. For example, if students have trouble understanding words that use prefixes and suffixes, you may want to assign that lesson to one student or to the class as a whole.

Practice Suggestions

Once students complete these lessons, the lessons should be reinforced with practice. Suggest that when students finish a lesson, they either form small groups or work individually to read a selection from a textbook or other assigned reading. Ask students to find examples of the kinds of words mentioned in an exercise as they read.

The Exercises

These exercises have been chosen because they provide direct help in understanding difficult words. Here is an overview of what the lessons are intended to accomplish.

Exercise 1 (page 86)
Direction Words

The words used in test questions or in other classroom situations may be unclear to students. This can lead to wrong answers on tests because students misunderstand what is asked. This lesson helps prevent misunderstandings by explaining what words in test questions mean. Once students understand these words, they can correctly answer the question.

Exercise 2 (page 87)
Context Clues: Part I

This is one of the most useful tools when it comes to understanding unfamiliar words. Students learn how to look for information about the meaning of words in surrounding words and sentences. They also learn how to find other usages of the unknown word that offer a wider base of information.

Exercise 3 (pages 88–89)
Context Clues: Part II

Often, unknown words can be understood by looking not just at the general context in which they appear, but also at other clues that authors provide. These may include definitions after words, restatements, meanings through example, and meanings through comparison and contrast.

Exercise 4 (pages 90–91)
Using Related Words to Find Meaning

One way readers can understand words is to recognize words within words. For example, students may not know the word *idealism*, but they probably know the meaning of the word *ideal*. Thus, using the word within the word can help students find a word's meaning.

Exercise 5 (pages 92–93)
Signal Words

Active readers can find clues to meaning through signal words. These words can alert readers to the introduction of new information, including a new subject, a series of steps, or a restatement of the author's main point. As students learn what words to look for and what each signals, they will become more proficient readers.

Exercise 6 (pages 94–95)
Prefixes and Suffixes

Another clue students can use is the prefix or suffix that is attached to an unknown word. For example, once students know the meanings of prefixes such as *dis-*, *re-*, *pre-*, and *un-*, students will be able to figure out the meaning of many unfamiliar words.

Apply What You Have Learned

The selections in the final review section of the Student Edition give students an opportunity to apply the reading strategies used in the text. To help students implement the strategies on their own, review the following guidelines with them.

Previewing Guidelines

- Write the selection title.

- List the subheadings.

- Write any information that the title and subheadings tell about what you will read.

- Write what you know about the topic.

- Look at any photos, charts, and maps in the selection. You should read the captions carefully, too.

As students continue their preview of the selection, have them answer the following questions.

- What do the first and last paragraphs tell you about the topic?

- What do the topic sentences tell you about the topic?

- How is the text organized?

- What do you think you will learn from your reading?

Guidelines for Taking Notes

Once students have completed their previews of a selection, work with them to choose an appropriate strategy and graphic organizer. Remind students that they can review all the strategies on the inside back cover of their books before they make a choice. Also remind students that they should read first and then take notes. Taking notes while reading can cause students to lose their place and their train of thought. If students need to refresh their memories about details in the selection, they can reread.

When they have finished taking their notes, remind students to review their work. This last review will ensure that students have understood their readings.

Assessment Guidelines

The following graphic demonstrates how the KWL Plus strategy might work for the selection "Florence Nightingale, Crusading Nurse." You might use this sample to help you assess students' graphic organizers. Notice that this student has used prior knowledge to generate prereading questions. These questions then helped the student build an understanding of the selection.

KWL CHART

K (What I know)	W (What I want to know)	L (What I've learned)
Florence Nightingale was a famous nurse.	Why did Nightingale become a nurse? How did she begin to change conditions in one hospital? What happened when Nightingale made these changes? What did Nightingale contribute to mathematics?	She wanted to help others. At the time, England and France were at war with Russia. Nightingale wanted to help her countrymen. She worked at a hospital with wounded soldiers. She was shocked to see the conditions at the hospital. She scrubbed the place, trained nurses, had better meals prepared for the patients. Within a year, the death rate was lower. She started a diagram we now call a pie chart.

Summary:

Florence Nightingale decided that she wanted to spend her life helping the sick. She went to school to study nursing. At the time she was to begin working, England and France were at war with Russia. Nightingale wanted to help her countrymen. She worked in a hospital with wounded soldiers. She did not like what she saw. She made changes. She scrubbed the place, trained nurses, and had better meals prepared for the patients. Her changes were successful. Within a year, the death rate was lower.

She contributed to mathematics by creating the pie chart. She used the charts to picture information she needed.

Reading Assessment

Effective readers tend to score well on state and standardized reading tests. You can also monitor, or have students monitor, their progress by using alternative forms of assessment. Here are some ways to gauge how well students understand and retain what they read:

Written Assessment

- **Portfolios** Student portfolios have gained in popularity because they enable a student to showcase the work he or she is proudest of. Self-selected student work can show a student's increasing ability in reading. Students might file a copy of their notes, a graphic organizer, and a summary for a selection.
- **Journals** Students can keep a journal in which they record reflections on their reading, vocabulary, and strategy use. Reviewing students' journals periodically and discussing them as time permits will help you assess students' understanding. Caution students that they should include in their journal only information they want to share.
- **Self-Assessment** Students generally are aware of their own strengths and weaknesses. Allowing them to use this knowledge can improve student comprehension and confidence. Discuss students' observations about their work. This can be done in weekly sessions as students complete a reading selection. Work on a plan both to acknowledge students' successes and to address their perceived weaknesses. This plan should focus on one or two weaknesses so that students will see progress.

Conferencing Assessment

- **Observations** Observing students' reading behaviors will provide additional insights into their ability to read strategically. Record your observations for each student. You might also wish to keep observation folders for all students to show their progress over time. Discuss your observations with students.
- **Interview Think-Alouds** Students who are having reading difficulties can benefit from an interview think-aloud. Ask a student to read a selection and, while reading, to explain what he or she is doing and thinking to understand the selection. Take notes while the student thinks aloud so that you do not have to interrupt the flow of the student's thoughts. Listen for an understanding of how the student previews; identifies the text structure, main points, and supporting details; and reviews the reading. Discuss effective and ineffective techniques with students. Once you have identified an area of difficulty, it will be easiesr to make a plan for improvement.

Reading Strategies and Test Preparation

In addition to helping students improve their comprehension of classroom assignments, the *Reading Strategies* series can also help students succeed on tests. The Apply It section in each selection helps students practice using reading strategies to check their comprehension. The Test Tips in these sections also offer students clues to understanding and correctly answering test questions. In addition, the Unit Reviews present reading selections and questions that can be used for review or as a test.

Preparing for Classroom Tests

Emphasize to students that when they use reading strategies, they will have done much of the work they need to do to prepare for tests. Display a completed graphic organizer and summary done by a student volunteer or by the class as a whole-class exercise.

Tell students that when it is time to prepare for a test, they can use their notes in two ways. First, they can review the notes. Second, they can write another summary based on the notes and compare it with the first summary they wrote. That comparison will help students review the main points of the reading. Because they already have written the main points and details of the reading, the review can concentrate on these facts, not on a range of unorganized notes or dimly remembered details.

Using Reading Strategies on a Standardized Test

Suggest to students that reading strategies are equally useful on the reading comprehension sections of standardized tests. Students should first preview the reading and the test questions, read carefully, take notes (if it is allowed during the test), and then think about what they have read. Approaching reading in this systematic way will help students answer the comprehension questions that follow a reading.

Practice Tests in the Student Edition

The Unit Reviews are designed to serve as an assessment tool. These reviews can be used both to assess students' understanding of the strategies and to help them prepare for a standardized test. Each review includes a test that measures each student's ability on both multiple-choice and short-answer questions. You might want to use a Unit Review to model how a student taking a reading comprehension test can approach a reading selection.

Test Tips

Throughout the Apply It sections in the units of the Student Edition are tips for successfully answering test questions. These Test Tips will help students on both classroom and standardized tests.

Some Test Tips deal with multiple-choice questions and offer hints on understanding the question being asked. Other Test Tips discuss answering short-answer and essay questions. For example, students are told that when a question asks them to choose the main idea of a selection, some of the answers may contain correct information, but only one choice is the *main idea*.

Many Test Tips, even if they are directed toward one type of question, have general applicability. For example, a tip that applies to understanding the direction line *make an inference* applies to both multiple-choice and short-answer questions.

The *Reading Strategies* series offers flexibility in test preparation. It can help students review for classroom tests and succeed on standardized tests.

Using the Graphic Organizers

On the following reproducible pages are graphic organizers that are designed to be used in teaching the lessons or in reinforcing the ways students understand text. You may want to use these graphics as guides when making larger copies on the board or on a large piece of chart paper. You may also use them to make transparencies for use with an overhead projector or for copies for individual students.

You can readily assess students' understanding of a selection by reviewing their graphic organizers. The organizers will give you a clear picture of what students have identified as the major points and supporting details of each selection. They will also show you how skillfully students preview and set questions for themselves that they then answer through reading.

Encourage students to keep their graphic organizers and any notes or summaries they create to understand a reading selection. These devices will help them review for a test. They can also be added to students' reading portfolios.

PACA (page T40)

In this graphic, students first fill in their predictions. They use the small boxes to check off correct predictions and note predictions that were either edited or added, and then they write the information that supports the prediction in the Support boxes.

DRTA (page T41)

In this graphic, students preview the selection and predict what they will read. Next, they take notes about their predictions and about other important information about the topic. Students then write a summary of the selection.

KWL Plus (page T42)

This graphic can be useful not only with the KWL Plus strategy selection but also in accessing students' prior knowledge on any subject before they read about it.

Concept Building (page T43)

This graphic works best for mathematics readings focused on one important idea. Students first write the concept, then define it, write the steps or supporting information that goes with it, and write a summary or work a mathematical problem to make sure they understand the concept.

Wheel-and-Spoke Diagram (page T44)

This is one of the most common graphic organizers for writing and reading. The main idea belongs in the center circle. The outside circles highlight the major points made in the writing. Underneath each circle, students can record the details that support each point. Students may add outside circles as needed.

Tree Map (page T45)

This graphic works well for a reading that is organized by time. In each box, students should record an important event, followed by the next box with the next important event. It can also be used to record a series of causes and effects.

Outline (page T46)

You can use this graphic to outline concepts in a mathematics selection.

Sequence Chart (page T47)

This graphic will work well in helping students solve math problems. They can isolate the steps needed to read, understand, and carry out the solution.

Name _____ Date _____

PACA

Prediction   **Support**

I used this strategy for: _____

Name _____   Date _____

DRTA

Preview	Take Notes	Review

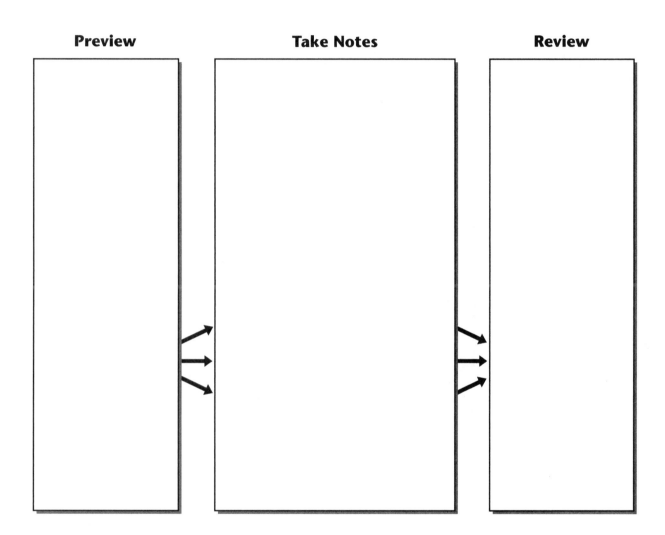

I used this strategy for: _____

Name _____   Date _____

KWL CHART

K (What I know)	W (What I want to know)	L (What I've learned)

I used this strategy for: _____

Name _____ Date _____

CONCEPT BUILDING

Concept

Definition or Formula

Evidence or Steps

Review or Examples

I used this strategy for: _____

Name _____ Date _____

WHEEL-AND-SPOKE DIAGRAM

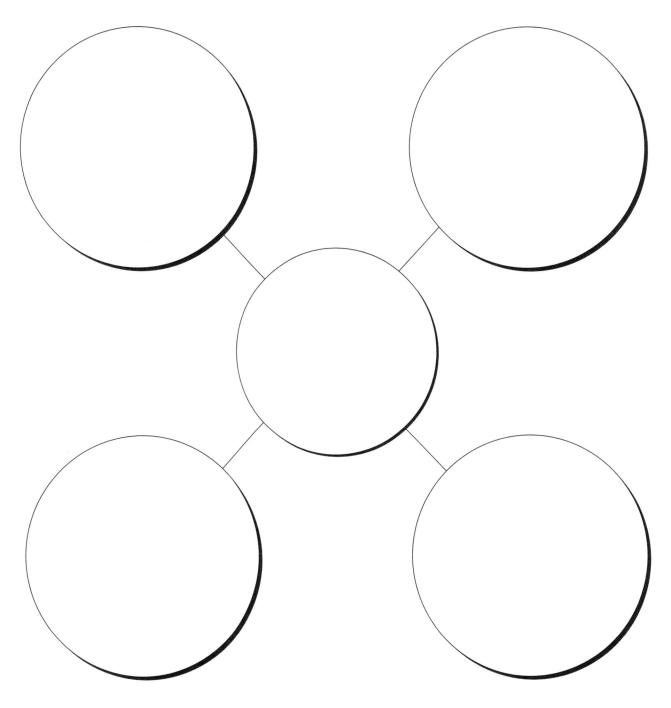

I used this strategy for: _____

Name _____   Date _____

TREE MAP

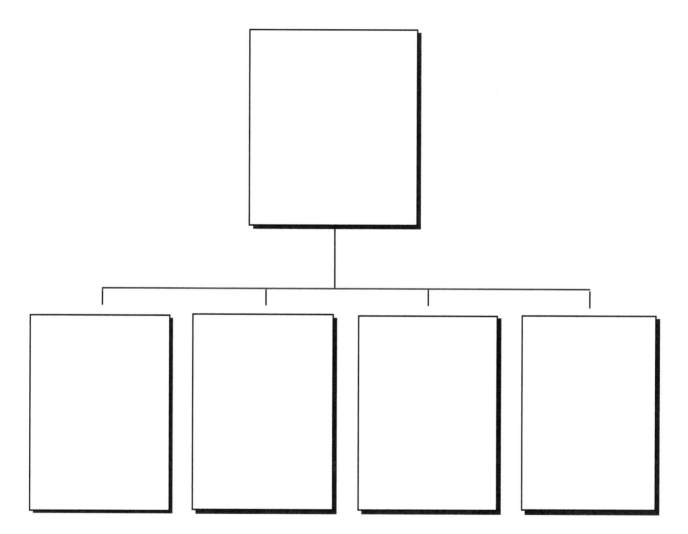

I used this strategy for: _____

Name _____   Date _____

OUTLINE

I. _____

  A. _____

    1. _____

    2. _____

  B. _____

    1. _____

    2. _____

      a. _____

      b. _____

      c. _____

II. _____

I used this strategy for: _____

Name _____ Date _____

SEQUENCE CHART

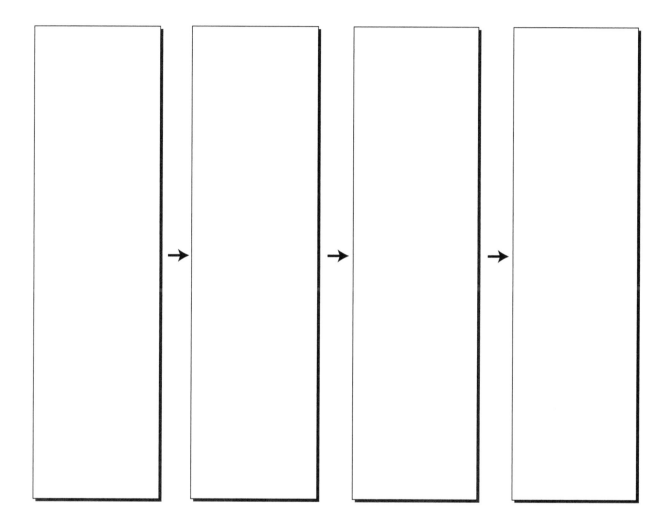

I used this strategy for: _____

Mathematics
Reading Strategies

Program Consultant
Dr. Kate Kinsella
San Francisco State University
San Francisco, California

GLOBE FEARON
Pearson Learning Group

Consultants

John Edwin Cowen, Ed.D.
Assistant Professor, Education/Reading;
Program Coordinator, Graduate M.A.T./
Elementary Education
School of Education
Fairleigh Dickinson University
Teaneck, New Jersey

Dr. Kate Kinsella
Dept. of Secondary Education and
Step to College Program
San Francisco State University
San Francisco, California

Reviewers

Bettye J. Birden, M.A.
Reading Specialist
McReynolds Middle School
Houston, TX

Sally Parker, M.A.
T.R. Smedberg Middle School/
Sheldon High School
Elk Grove, Unified School District
Elk Grove, CA

Georgeanne Herbeck
District Supervisor, Elementary Education
Perth Amboy, NJ

Kenneth J. Ratti
Science Department Chairman
Vaca Peña Middle School
Vacaville, CA

Supervising Editor: Lynn W. Kloss
Senior Editor: Renée E. Beach
Editorial Assistant: Jennifer Watts
Writers: Sandra Widener, Terri Flynn-Nason
Production Editor: Laura Benford-Sullivan
Cover and Interior Design: Sharon Scannell
Electronic Page Production: Linda Bierniak
Manufacturing Supervisor: Mark Cirillo

Photo Credits
p. 7: Richard Hutchins, Photo Researchers; p. 8: Ken Cavanaugh, Photo Researchers; p. 11: Spencer Grant, Photo Researchers; p. 17: Jeff Greenberg, Photo Researchers; p. 26: Silver Burdett Ginn; p. 27: Silver Burdett Ginn; p. 47: NBA Entertainment; p. 50: (top) David Seelig, Allsport; p. 50: (bottom) Jed Jacobsohn, Allsport; p. 54: Jim Wilson, NYT Pictures; p. 103: Corbis/Bettmann; p. 107: Courtesy of Kenneth Granderson

ISBN: 0-130-23791-4
Printed in the United States of America
4 5 6 7 8 9 10   06 05 04 03 02

1-800-321-3106
www.pearsonlearning.com

Contents

To the Student

The Hows and Whys of Reading

Think of a story that you've read. Maybe it was about someone's exciting adventure. What did you want to know about the story? What kinds of questions did you ask to get that information?

If you were reading an adventure story, you probably wanted to know *who* the characters were and *when* and *where* they were going. These questions are very helpful when reading *literary text,* which includes things like short stories, novels, plays, and myths. They all tell a story.

There is another kind of writing that is called *informational text.* This kind of writing informs the reader by giving opinions, explanations, reasons, facts, and examples about a certain topic. Things like chapters in a textbook and newspaper articles are considered informational text, so you are already familiar with this type of writing.

Good Questions for Literary Text	Good Questions for Informational Text
who	how
when	what
where	why

Think back to an example of a literary text you've read. How are the questions you ask about a story different from the ones you ask when you read a chapter in your mathematics book? In a mathematics book, the questions *how, what,* and *why* are a great way to ask the "big" questions to get the information you are looking for. You might even start by changing the bold type headings and topic sentences into questions that begin with *how, what,* and *why.* Since *who, where,* and *when* questions can be answered with a simple fact or one-word answer, they are not as useful when reading informational text. Look at the following example:

Heading		Question
Promoting Economic Growth	*becomes*	How can you promote economic growth?
Causes of Earthquakes	*becomes*	What causes earthquakes?
The Protests Affect U.S. Policy	*becomes*	Why do the protests affect U.S. policy?

These are examples of "big" questions. It is by asking these big questions and by answering them by reading, that you will get the most out of the informational texts that you read.

Using Reading Strategies

Although you may not know it, you may already use a strategy when you read. Here's an example. You look at a magazine cover. A headline catches your eye. You see a picture of a musician or style of clothing you like. Then you look at the table of contents. Does an article sound interesting? If it does, you turn to that page. You look at a photograph in the article. Then you read the caption under it. You read the article. After you read, you think about what you have read. You have just used a reading strategy.

A reading strategy is a plan that helps you understand the information you read. The reading strategies in this book can help you understand readings in language arts, social studies, science, and math. They can also help you understand things you read in your life outside of school or at a job. You will be able to link what you are reading to what you already know. Reading strategies will also help you remember what you read.

Becoming an Active Reader

When you use a strategy for reading, you take an active part in reading. You respond to the reading with thoughts, questions, and ideas. You also respond by taking notes or summarizing what you read. Finally, you think about what you read. What these steps have in common is that you are involved with what you are reading.

Steps of the Strategies

Although different strategies work well for different kinds of reading, all the strategies in this book have four steps in common. You preview. Then you read and take notes. Finally, you review. Below is a drawing of the steps of the reading strategies.

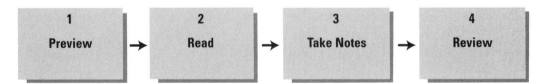

First, preview what you will read. In every strategy, you preview what you will read. When you preview, you think about what you already know about the topic. You also look for clues about what you will learn.

Here are the steps to use when you preview:

1. Look at the title. What clues does it give you about the topic?

2. Look at the illustrations or diagrams and read the captions. Often, major points are illustrated.

3. Read the first paragraph. It may include a summary of what is to come.

4. Read the last paragraph. It may sum up the writer's main points.

5. Read the first sentence of every paragraph. It will give you hints on what you will read.

Second, read carefully. As you read, think about what you are reading. What is the author telling you? Do you understand all of the words you are reading? Look for clues that the author has given you.

Third, take notes. The kind of notes you take will vary depending on what you are reading. A researcher found that students remember only 5 to 34 percent of the information they don't take notes on. When you take notes, you put information in your own words. That helps the information stay in your mind.

Fourth, review what you have read. You may review a section in a math textbook by working problems to see if you understand the concept. Often, though, you will want to write a summary. When you write a summary, you put the author's thoughts into your own words. You review the main points of the reading and the details that support these main points.

Choosing a Strategy

There are a variety of strategies in this book because people learn—and read—in different ways. After trying different strategies, you might find that one always works best for you. You may also find that one strategy works better on one type of reading. For example, one strategy might work well on an article on how to make a poster. Another strategy might work well on a debate about movie ratings.

Experiment with these strategies. You'll find that you can use them on any reading you have, both in school and out of school. You'll also find that they'll help you make sense of your reading—and remember it!

Reading in Mathematics

When you read the statistics in the sports section of the newspaper, you are reading mathematics. When you read a recipe, you are reading mathematics. When you figure out how much it will cost you to buy a car, you are reading mathematics. As you can see, mathematics reading goes far beyond your textbooks.

How Mathematics Reading Is Organized

Reading mathematics is different from other kinds of reading. When you read mathematics, you must pay attention to symbols, numbers, and equations. You must also make sure you understand one topic before you go on to the next. Much of mathematics builds on what you already know. If you don't learn one topic, you will find the next topic very difficult. Recognizing patterns in mathematics reading will help you understand what you read. Here are some common patterns you may see.

Diagrams and Graphs. In mathematics, sometimes a diagram or graph represents the main point of the reading. The text before and after the diagram or graph explains it. When you see this pattern, you know that you must pay attention to the graph or diagram. You can better understand what the text is saying if you redraw the diagram yourself and write an explanation of the concept.

Obtuse Angles

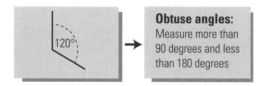

Formulas and Equations. Often, a mathematics lesson will be based on equations and formulas. Carefully look at each symbol. Once you know each symbol's meaning, you can move on. When you see equations and formulas, it is also a clue that you need to be able to use the formula before you move on. Prove to yourself you understand it by working problems based on either the formula or the equation.

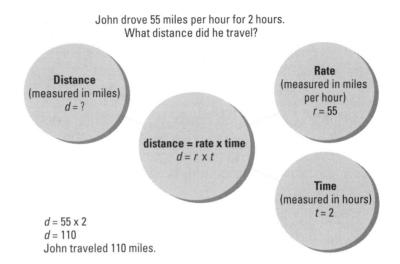

John drove 55 miles per hour for 2 hours.
What distance did he travel?

Distance
(measured in miles)
$d = ?$

distance = rate x time
$d = r \times t$

Rate
(measured in miles per hour)
$r = 55$

Time
(measured in hours)
$t = 2$

$d = 55 \times 2$
$d = 110$
John traveled 110 miles.

Steps of a Process. Much of mathematics reading describes a process. For example, you might read the instructions from your bank on balancing your checking account. In a textbook, you might read the steps of the process for multiplying decimals. When you see this pattern, you know to look for the next step as you read. Here are two tips to getting the most out of this pattern. First, rewrite the steps in your own words, so you know you understand them. Second, try several examples to make sure you understand the process.

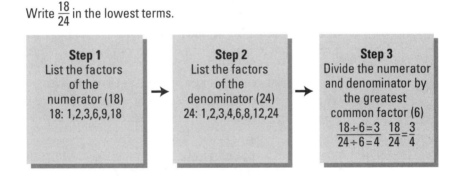

Write $\frac{18}{24}$ in the lowest terms.

Step 1
List the factors of the numerator (18)
18: 1,2,3,6,9,18

Step 2
List the factors of the denominator (24)
24: 1,2,3,4,6,8,12,24

Step 3
Divide the numerator and denominator by the greatest common factor (6)
$\frac{18 \div 6 = 3}{24 \div 6 = 4}$ $\frac{18}{24} = \frac{3}{4}$

Getting the Most from Your Reading

If you can recognize the way a reading is organized, you will be better able to understand what you read. You will be able to think about what kind of information might be next and how all the points in the reading fit together. Drawing word maps like the ones on these two pages can show you these patterns. Thinking about how a reading is organized can help you understand—and remember—what you read.

Unit 1 Strategy: **PACA**

Understand It...... Active readers often use a reading strategy called PACA. PACA stands for **P**redicting **A**nd **C**onfirming **A**ctivity. The strategy is based on the idea that a reader can often predict what a selection will be about. After you make a prediction, look for information that confirms you are right—or wrong. What you find out can help you understand your reading.

PACA is a good strategy to use when you know enough about what you are reading to make a prediction about it. When you predict and then check your prediction, you become an active reader. Active readers get more out of reading because they think about what they read.

Try It.............. The following selection shows a debate about school uniforms. Maybe you have an opinion on the issue. Because you have heard about the topic, the PACA strategy is a good one to use. Think about what you already know about school uniforms. You may be able to predict what people on both sides of the debate might think. Try the PACA method with this student.

Step 1. Predict what you will read.

When you predict, you preview the writing to see what it is about. The student looked at the titles of these essays. They told her the selection was a debate about whether students should wear uniforms to school. She thought about what she already knew about the debate over uniforms.

We don't have school uniforms, but I know some kids who wear them to school. What do they think about them? Do they mind wearing them? What would wearing a uniform be like? How would I feel? Maybe I'd like not having to think about what to put on every morning. Maybe I'd hate the way a uniform looked.

The student then looked quickly at the writing. She wrote a prediction about what the reasons for and against school uniforms might be. Here is the beginning of her PACA chart. Add your own predictions to the chart.

Predictions	Support
the person who is against school uniforms will write that wearing uniforms will cost more	
the person who is for uniforms likes the uniform she wears	
the person who is for uniforms will write that uniforms make dressing easier	
the person who is against uniforms will write that uniforms destroy being individual	

Step 2. Read and confirm your predictions.

Keep your predictions close at hand when you read. First, when you see information that confirms one prediction, make a check mark next to it. Second, when you find points in the writing you did not predict, write them and draw a star next to each one. Finally, cross out predictions that are wrong to avoid confusion.

After she began reading, the student began marking and revising her list of predictions. Remember that you wrote predictions too. If they turn out to be wrong, change them.

Predictions	Support
the person who is against school uniforms will write that wearing uniforms will cost more ✓	
~~the person who is for uniforms likes the uniform she wears~~	
the person who is for uniforms will write that uniforms make dressing easier ✓	
the person who is against uniforms will write that uniforms destroy being individual ✓	

Debate: Should Schools Require Uniforms?

Against Uniforms: By Kate Monahan

When I think of having to wear uniforms to school, my heart just sinks. It's bad enough with all the rules we have to follow. I wouldn't be surprised if lots of people dropped out.

There are many reasons why making students wear uniforms is a terrible idea. For one, it would end up costing more. Even if you had uniforms to wear to school, you would still need clothes for the rest of the time. You'd need two sets of clothes, and that gets expensive.

Should students really be able to choose?

Some people say that violence would stop if we wore uniforms. I think that's stupid. If people are going to fight, they're going to fight. What people are wearing isn't going to stop them from fighting. They'll just find another reason.

It's the same with people who say that unpopular kids can't keep up and uniforms will make everyone equal. That doesn't matter. If someone is cool, he won't get picked on, even if his clothes aren't the best. But if someone is not cool, the best clothes on the planet will not keep him from being made fun of. Making us wear certain types of clothes won't make any difference.

What I'd really like to know is what happened to the First Amendment to the Constitution. Doesn't that say everyone has freedom of speech? Well, my freedom of speech is in how I dress. This is a **constitutional** wrong! I have a right to express myself. Clothes are how I do that.

I thought school was supposed to teach students how to make choices. Making us wear uniforms says that adults think we can't make good choices. It says that adults don't want to give us the chance to *learn* how to make good choices. Forcing us to wear uniforms also shows that adults don't trust us.

I don't want to go to a school that forces everyone to be the same. I think it will create boring people who don't question anything and who blindly accept anything they are told. It is my civil right to wear what I want!

For Uniforms: By Edie Hamilton

As a student who would have to wear uniforms if the school board votes for them, I think I have a right to speak. There are several reasons I think having school uniforms is a great idea.

First, parents and students spend way too much money on school clothes. Everyone has to have the latest shoes, the latest jeans, the latest whatever, and that means lots of money. Not everyone has that kind of money. If we had

Don't uniforms mean a kind of equality?

uniforms, no one would be able to look down on someone because she didn't have the right clothes.

I also think that if we wore uniforms, there would be less gang violence. Right now, everyone is on edge. We never know when someone is going to wear clothes that will end up with people fighting over gang colors. Even though the school tries to stop it, teachers don't always know what different kinds of clothing mean.

> I think if everyone wore uniforms, people would think of school more seriously. It would be like a job, not a social place. You would know that when you put on your uniform, it was time to think about school.
>
> I know some people think choosing what to wear to school is a matter of self-expression. To those people, I say, "Get a life!" It's what's inside that counts. You can express yourself by how you act. Most important, you can express yourself by what you produce in school.
>
> If we had uniforms, I think we'd be much better off. We would have to spend less money on clothes. There wouldn't be as much violence. People would be able to focus on what's really important: learning.

Step 3. Support your predictions.

Look at what you wrote in your chart. Make notes by each point to make sure it sticks in your mind. Maybe you'll find supporting arguments for the points you wrote and for the main points the debaters made. Write this evidence in the Support column of your chart.

Here is how the student began adding to her predictions.

Predictions	Support
the person who is against school uniforms will write that wearing uniforms will cost more ✓	uniforms are expensive need clothes for home as well as school
~~the person who is for uniforms likes the uniform she wears~~	
the person who is for uniforms will write that uniforms make dressing easier ✓	less pressure on everyone to have the latest fashionwear
the person who is against uniforms will write that uniforms destroy being individual ✓	destroys the right to express oneself

Apply It.. . . . . Use the PACA strategy with a reading assignment you have. Look it over. What do the headings tell you about the topic? What do you already know about it? Write your predictions in your own PACA chart.

Then read the assignment, looking for information about your predictions. When you see information that confirms a prediction, make a check mark next to it. When you see points you did not predict, write them and put a star in front of each one. Cross out predictions that are wrong. Finally, write in the evidence or examples that support each point. You should now have a good review of the important points in your reading assignment.

Lesson 1

Number Sense: Number Patterns

Understand It...... Most people have a morning routine. They follow the same pattern every morning. A pattern is anything that occurs in a repeated order, or sequence. There are many different kinds of patterns. Floor tiles often have a pattern. House numbers on a street have a pattern. The route a school bus takes has a pattern. Even your school day has a pattern.

Try It.............. This selection explores number patterns. Use the PACA strategy to help you understand the reading. Start by predicting what you will learn. Think about all the kinds of number patterns you know.

On a separate piece of paper, draw your own PACA chart like the one below. Record your predictions in the Predictions column of the chart. Then read the selection. After you read, confirm or revise your predictions. If your reading confirms a prediction, write a check mark in the left column. If you need to add or revise a prediction, write a star in the left column. Finally, write information that supports all of these points in the Support column.

Strategy Tip
Look at the title and subheadings of the selection as you preview it. What do you think you will learn? Record your predictions in your PACA chart.

Predictions	Support

Vocabulary Tip
Do you know what a *sequence* is? Look at the sentences that follow the word. The sentence gives the meaning of the term.

Number Patterns

Leonardo Fibonacci was a great European mathematician. In the 13th century, he identified this number **sequence**:

1, 1, 2, 3, 5, 8, 13, ...

The Fibonacci sequence is a number pattern. The terms that make up the pattern have a relationship. In this relationship the pattern does not change. It goes on and on.

Look at the first two terms of the Fibonacci sequence. They are 1 and 1. Look at the third term. How are 1 and 1 related to 2? Look at the second and third terms. How are 1 and 2 related to 3? Look at the third and fourth terms. How are 2 and 3 related to 5? Each term is the sum of the two terms that come before it. This pattern does not change. It is constant.

The square of a series of whole numbers has a different kind of pattern. Look at the chart that follows. Study each line. Look for a constant relationship.

$$1^2 = 1$$
$$2^2 = 4 = 1 + 3$$
$$3^2 = 9 = 1 + 3 + 5$$
$$4^2 = 16 = 1 + 3 + 5 + 7$$
$$5^2 = 25 = 1 + 3 + 5 + 7 + 9$$

Do you see the pattern? The value of 1^2 is the first odd number, or 1. The value of 2^2 is the sum of the first two odd numbers, or 4. The value of 3^2 is the sum of the first three odd numbers, or 9. You can use that addition pattern to find the square of any whole number. The value of 7^2 is the sum of the first seven odd numbers. What is that value?

Number Patterns in Daily Life

Many businesses use number patterns to predict their future sales. They record yearly sales information. They review the information and identify patterns. Then they make predictions based on these patterns.

Maggie's Framing Company sells picture frames. The company has been in business for three years. During the first year, the company sold 3,208 picture frames. In the second year, the company sold 3,528 frames. During the third year, 4,056 frames were sold.

Vocabulary Tip

Notice that the word *data* is in bold type. Sometimes, writers define words by using examples. Here, the writer defines *data* by giving you examples in the three sentences before the word is used.

The company owner analyzed that **data**. She discovered that between the first and second years, sales increased by 10 percent. Between the second and third years, the company's sales increased by 15 percent. The owner used that trend to make predictions about sales for the next two years. She predicted that sales would increase by 20 percent in the fourth year and by 25 percent in the fifth year. The predictions helped her plan for the future. She hired more workers to make the frames. She also hired more salesclerks. Now she will be able to keep up with increased demand for her unusual frames.

Number patterns help communities plan for the future, too. Town officials gather information about their community's population. They look for patterns in the data. Sometimes the number patterns show a steady increase in population. That

Number patterns can help determine how many firefighters a city needs.

Number Sense:
Number Patterns

means more people will need town services. Officials must make plans for future growth. They might need to hire more firefighters or build more schools. Sometimes the number patterns show a steady decrease in population. Fewer people will need town services. Officials make plans to reduce the number of town employees or even to close schools.

Number patterns have probably led to predictions about your community. The next time you see a new traffic light, street sign, or improved road, think of a number pattern!

Now look back at the predictions you made. Revise the ones that were incorrect. Add information you didn't predict. Write stars next to any predictions that you added or revised. Then be sure to add information that supports your predictions.

Apply It. . . . . To check your understanding of the selection, circle the best answer to each of the following questions.

1. All number patterns involve
    a. a sum.
    b. multiplication.
    c. a relationship.
    d. a steady decrease.

2. The tone of this selection is
    a. humorous.
    b. sad.
    c. mysterious.
    d. informative.

Test Tip

To correctly answer question 3, you must identify a cause-and-effect relationship. The question states the cause: Officials see a new number pattern. The correct answer identifies what happens—the effect—as a result of the cause.

3. Suppose your town government notices that the population of the town is falling. What might happen after officials see this number pattern?
    a. Voters might elect a new mayor.
    b. The number of firefighters might be reduced.
    c. An old school might be repainted.
    d. Your class might go on a field trip.

4. What is data?
    a. a prediction
    b. a collection of information
    c. the manager of a company
    d. a future occurrence

5. The sequence 1, 19, 5, 2, 33, … is *not* a number pattern because the terms
   a. do not show a constant relationship.
   b. are steadily increasing.
   c. increase and then decrease.
   d. change in the same manner.

Use the lines below to write your answers for numbers 6 and 7. You can use your PACA notes to help you.

6. Look at the following number pattern: 11, 13, 17, 25, …. Explain how to identify the next three terms in the pattern.

Answers should describe comparing the first and second terms, the second and third terms, the third and fourth terms, and so on. The comparisons show that the first term is increased by 2 to yield the second term. The second term is increased by 4 or 2^2 to yield the third term. The third term is increased by 8 or 2^3 to yield the fourth term. For each two numbers in the sequence, the difference doubles. Following that pattern, the next three terms in the sequence are 41, 73, and 137.

7. Suppose that number patterns show that the population of your community will increase by 1,000 people each year for the next ten years. What should be done to prepare for that growth? Write a letter to town officials describing three things that must be changed.

Answers will vary but may include building additional schools; increasing the size of service departments such as the police, fire, or sanitation departments; and building more roads.

Lesson 2

Numerical Operations: Russian Peasant Multiplication Method

Understand It...... Can you find the product of two factors without multiplying? You can if you know the Russian Peasant Multiplication Method. In this selection, you will learn this multiplication process. Use the PACA strategy to help you understand the steps.

Try It.............. Begin by drawing a PACA chart like the one shown below. Use what you know about multiplication to help you make predictions. Write your predictions in the Predictions column of the chart. Revise or confirm your predictions after you read. Write evidence that supports your predictions in the support column.

Predictions	Support

Russian Peasant Multiplication Method

Yesterday, 26 boxes of compact discs were delivered to Al's Music Shop. Each box holds 35 CDs. Al needs to label each disc. The store manager, Beth, wants to know how many labels she needs. She does this by finding the product of 26 and 35. However, Beth does not multiply to find the answer. Instead, she makes two columns. Beth marks one column *Halve* and the other column *Double*. Then she puts the first factor in the first column and the second factor in the second column.

Halve	Double
26	35

Next, Beth finds one-half of 26. She writes 13 in the first column. She doubles 35 and writes 70 in the second column.

Halve	Double
26	35
13	70

Beth continues finding half of each amount in the first column. (If one-half of a number is a whole number and a decimal, she **omits** the decimal.) In the second column, Beth continues doubling numbers. She repeats this process until the last entry in the first column is 1. Finally, her columns look like this:

Halve	Double
26	35
13	70
6	140
3	280
1	560

Now, Beth circles all the even numbers in the first column. She circles 26 and 6. She crosses out the numbers directly across from the circled numbers, or 35 and 140. Finally, Beth adds the remaining numbers in the second column. She finds that the sum of 70 + 280 + 560 is 910. Beth goes to the storeroom to get 910 labels.

Halve	Double
⊙26	~~35~~
13	70
⊙6	~~140~~
3	280
1	<u>560</u>
	910

How Many Ice Cream Cones Are Needed?

During the month of July, Sweet Treat Ice Cream store used 52 boxes of ice cream cones. Each box contained 48 cones. You can use the Russian Peasant Multiplication Method to find the total number of cones used during July. Begin by making two columns. Label the first column *Halve* and the second column *Double*. Write 52 in the first column. Write 48 in the second column.

Do you remember what to do next? Find one-half of 52, or 26. Write 26 in the first column. Across from it, write 96, which is 48 doubled. Continue until the last entry in the first column is 1. (Remember, if half of a number is a whole number and decimal, omit the decimal.)

Now, circle all the even numbers in the first column. Cross out the numbers directly across from them in the second column. Add the remaining doubles. You should find that the Sweet Treat Ice Cream store used 2,496 cones during July.

Which Method Do You Prefer?

You probably learned to multiply to find a product. In the Russian Peasant Multiplication Method, you halve, double, and add to find a product. Although the method may be new to you, it will give you what you are looking for—the correct answer! So the next time you need to find the product of two factors, try this new method instead of multiplying.

Strategy Tip

As you preview the selection, notice the two subheadings: "How Many Ice Cream Cones Are Needed?" and "Which Method Do You Prefer?" What do you think these sections will be about?

Now that you have finished reading the selection, complete your PACA chart with information you have learned. Instead of writing a summary of the selection, create a problem and solve it. That will prove that you understand the Russian Peasant Multiplication Method.

Numerical Operations:
Russian Peasant Multiplication Method

Apply It. . . . . To check your understanding of the selection, circle the best answer to each of the following questions.

1. The author wrote this selection to
   a. explain how addition and multiplication are related.
   b. explore customs from other cultures.
   c. analyze life in Russia.
   d. describe the steps in a mathematical process.

2. When you use the Russian Peasant Multiplication Method, what should you do first?
   a. Set up a multiplication problem.
   b. Make two columns.
   c. Add the factors.
   d. Find the difference of the factors.

3. Why did Beth get 910 labels from the storeroom?
   a. There were 910 CDs.
   b. She expected 910 customers that month.
   c. A delivery of 910 boxes had just arrived.
   d. She had to fill 910 orders.

Test Tip

Reviewing the examples and the charts in the selection can help you find the answer to question 4.

4. What is the next step after circling all the even numbers in the first column?
   a. Find the product of the remaining numbers.
   b. Circle the odd numbers in the second column.
   c. Cross out the numbers directly across from them.
   d. Find the sum of all the numbers in the second column.

Use the lines below to write your answers for numbers 5 and 6. Use your PACA chart to help you.

5. Write a letter to a friend that explains the Russian Peasant Multiplication Method. Make up a problem and draw a chart to explain the process.

   Letters should describe the following: making two columns, recording the factors, finding one half of each entry in the first column, doubling the values in the second column, circling the even numbers in the first column, crossing out the numbers directly across from the circled numbers, and finding the sum of the remaining numbers in the second column.

6. Suppose you need to find the product of two numbers. Which process would you use? Explain your choice.

   Answers will vary but should include an explanation for the choice students have made.

Problem Solving:
Lesson 3 Finding Relevant Information

Understand It...... Anyone who has ever taken a math class has solved word problems. A word problem describes a situation. It asks a question about the situation. To answer the question, the reader must perform some type of calculation. In this selection you will learn how to read—and solve—word problems.

Try It.............. Since you probably know something about word problems, PACA is a good reading strategy to use. Draw a PACA chart like the one below on a separate sheet of paper. First, preview the selection and predict what you will learn. Record your predictions in the Predictions column of your chart. Then read the selection. After reading, confirm or revise your predictions. Add a check mark next to predictions you confirm. Write stars next to predictions you add or revise. Finally, write details that support your predictions in the Support column.

Strategy Tip

Think about how you have solved word problems in math. What did you do first? Next? Use these ideas to make predictions on what this selection will be about.

Predictions	Support

Finding Relevant Information

Every word problem asks a question. Every word problem contains information. The reader must use the information in the problem to answer that question. Some of the information is **relevant**, or related, to the problem. Some of the information is not relevant—that is, it is unnecessary. A good problem solver focuses on relevant information. A good problem solver has a plan for finding the correct answer.

Vocabulary Tip

Do you know what *relevant* means? Look at the words that follow the term. They contain a synonym for *relevant*. What is the synonym?

Create a Plan

- The first step in the plan is to read the problem carefully. Determine what you are being asked to find out. This is the question you must answer.

- Then make a list of all the information contained in the problem. Include everything.

How could a plan help these students?

Problem Solving:
Finding Relevant Information

Strategy Tip

This selection has two kinds of lists: bulleted lists, or lists with dots, and numbered lists. Lists often show important information. Pay attention to them when you preview a selection.

- Next, look over your list. Think about what you are being asked to find out. Cross out any information in your list that is not relevant to the question. Circle the information that will help you answer the question.

- Finally, use the relevant information to solve the problem. Complete the steps to find the answer.

Use this plan to solve the following word problem:

The Sweater Shop has been in business for 27 years. The shop has been so busy that the owners had to hire three more workers. If business continues to be this good, the owners might open another store. December was the busiest month in the history of the shop. Sales for the month totaled $34,528. If this was $9,017 more than the sales for the previous month, what was November's sales total?

Put Your Plan to Work

Now think about what the problem asks you to find out. The last sentence of the problem contains this question. You must determine the sales total for November.

Next, make a list of all the information contained in the problem. Your list should look like this:

1. The shop has been in business for 27 years.

2. The owners hired three new workers.

3. The owners are thinking about opening another store.

4. December was the busiest month in the history of the shop.

5. December sales totaled $34,528.

6. December's sales total was $9,017 more than the sales for the previous month.

Review the list. Think about the question. What information will not help you find November's sales total? Items 1, 2, 3, and 4 are not relevant. Cross them out. Look at items 5 and 6. They will help you find November's sales total. Circle these items.

Use the circled items to solve the word problem. Because December's total was *more* than November's total, you need to set up a subtraction problem. You will subtract $9,017 from $34,528. The answer is $25,511. This means that the sales total for November was $25,511.

You can use this plan to solve any kind of word problem. It will help you collect and organize information. It will also help you focus on what information is relevant to the problem.

Now that you have finished reading the selection, revise or change any predictions that were incorrect. Mark these predictions with a star. Then add details that support your predictions in the Support column.

Apply It. . . . . To check your understanding of the selection, circle the best answer to each question below.

1. What is the first thing to do after reading a problem?
   a. Set up a math problem.
   b. Decide what you are being asked to find out.
   c. Perform the calculations.
   d. Make a list of all the information contained in the problem.

2. Which word in the selection is an antonym, or opposite, of *relevant*?
   a. necessary
   b. important
   c. unnecessary
   d. both a and b

3. Why is it important to make a list of information before solving a problem?
   a. to check the answer to the problem
   b. to see how quickly you can solve the problem
   c. to see which parts of the problem are relevant
   d. to take out relevant information

4. What is the author's purpose for writing this selection?
   a. to develop people's interest in mathematics
   b. to describe a successful business
   c. to show how math is used in everyday life
   d. to describe a plan for solving word problems

Use the lines below to write your answers for numbers 5 and 6. You can use your PACA chart to help you.

5. Describe a plan you would use to solve a word problem.

Answers will vary but should describe the plan detailed in the reading.

_____

6. Create a new word problem about food sales in the cafeteria or some other topic. On another piece of paper, show how to use the problem-solving plan to find its solution.

Problems will vary. Solutions should identify the steps described in the selection.

_____

_____

_____

Lesson 4

Problem Solving: Guess and Check

Understand It...... This reading is about a problem-solving method called guess and check. You can use guess and check to figure out word problems in math class. You can also use it in many real-life situations. Use the PACA strategy to help you remember the main points of this selection.

Try It.............. Think about the word *guess* in the title. A guess is a kind of prediction. When you preview the reading, you'll notice a series of steps. They are clues to the selection's main points.

Copy the PACA chart on another sheet of paper. Then make Predictions about the kind of information the selection contains. Think about your predictions as you read. When you're finished reading, you will confirm your predictions.

Strategy Tip

Use your experiences with word problems when making your predictions.

Predictions	Support

Vocabulary Tip

Most words have more than one meaning. Think about the way *key* is used in this selection. How does the meaning differ from the way *key* is used in the sentence "Josh lost his house key"?

Guess and Check

Have you ever entered a contest in which you had to guess how many items were in a container? You might have guessed how many jelly beans were in a glass jug. To win, you needed to make a good guess.

Solving certain kinds of word problems also requires making a good guess. You check your guess. If you are wrong, you make an adjustment. You guess again. Often, you need to make a series of guesses until you find the solution. That problem-solving method is called *guess and check*.

The **key** to using the method well is making good guesses. You base a good guess on known facts. You think about what you need to figure out. You think about what you already know. You use the information to make a good guess. You check your guess. If it is wrong, you make another guess.

You can use guess and check to solve the following problem:

The Hawks soccer team has 15 members. The team played two dozen games last season. Three of the games ended in a tie. The team won twice as many games as it lost. How many games did the Hawks lose last season?

Strategy Tip

Add a prediction about each of these three subheadings to your PACA chart.

Step 1: Identify What You Need to Find

Read the problem again. What are you being asked to find out? The last sentence of the problem contains that information. You must determine the number of games the Hawks lost last season.

Step 2: Identify What You Know

Go back to the problem. Underline the facts given. You need some, but not all, of that information to find a solution. Facts contained in this problem include the following:

- The team has 15 members.
- The team played 2 dozen, or 24, games last season.
- Three games ended in a tie.
- The team won twice as many games as it lost

Step 3: Use What You Know to Make a Guess

You know the team played 24 games. Three games ended in a tie. That means the total number of games won or lost was 24 – 3, or 21. Use the facts to make a guess.

Perhaps you guess that the team lost 6 games. Check your guess. According to the problem, the team won twice as many games as it lost. According to your guess, the team won 12 games and lost 6. Does 12 + 6 equal 21, which is the total number of games won or lost? No. Therefore, you must guess again.

Try a higher number, such as 7. That means the team won 14 games and lost 7. Does 14 + 7 equal 21? Yes! Therefore, the solution is 7.

As you can see, this problem-solving method involves much more than random guessing. When you use guess and check, you perform a series of steps. Each step leads you closer to a solution. The next time you need to solve a math word problem, try using the guess-and-check method.

Now that you have finished reading about guess and check, look at your PACA chart. Put check marks next to the predictions that you confirmed. Then revise or add to your predictions. Note important points that you had not thought of. Add them to your list of predictions. Finally, add support for each prediction.

Apply It. . . . . To check your understanding of the selection, circle the best answer to each question below.

1. What is guess and check?
   a. a math game
   b. a contest
   c. a math problem
   d. a problem-solving method

Problem Solving: Guess and Check

Test Tip

The steps in the problem-solving process must be done in a certain sequence. In question 2, you need to put two of the steps in the correct order.

2. According to the selection, what should you do after reading the problem?
   a. List what you know.
   b. Write the problem on a sheet of paper.
   c. Identify what you need to find out.
   d. Make a guess.

3. A good guess is
   a. based on facts.
   b. made quickly.
   c. a guess that is correct.
   d. a guess that everybody agrees on.

4. What is the author's purpose for writing this selection?
   a. to show that math is fun
   b. to teach a process
   c. to entertain others
   d. to convince students that math is important

5. What is the tone of the selection?
   a. humorous
   b. formal
   c. informative
   d. sad

Use the lines below to write your answers for numbers 6 and 7. Use your PACA chart to help you.

6. Al is six years older than Joe. Their combined ages equal 34. Explain how you could use guess and check to figure out Al's age. (Hint: Begin by listing pairs of numbers whose sum is 34. Then try those pairs to see which one makes sense.)

Answers should describe the three steps outlined in the selection to find that Al is 20 years old and Joe is 14 years old.

7. How are the guess-and-check method and the PACA strategy similar?

Answers should demonstrate an understanding of the key points of each strategy. In both strategies, students make guesses, or predictions. Then they read or try out their predictions to find out if they were correct.

Unit 1 Review: **PACA**

In this unit, you have practiced using the PACA reading strategy. Use this strategy when you read the selection below. Use a separate sheet of paper to draw a chart, take notes, and summarize what you learn.

Hint *Remember that all reading strategies have activities for before, during, and after reading. To review these steps, look at the inside back cover of this book.*

Units of Measure

Imagine you are a person living long ago. You want to measure something. Yet there are no measuring devices. What do you do?

What most ancient people did was use something they did know: themselves. In Egypt, people measured using a *cubit*. This was the average length from a man's elbow to the tip of his middle finger.

The Romans were the first to use the *foot* as a measure. It was the length of a grown man's foot. The Romans also added the mile as a measurement. A mile was the distance a Roman soldier could go in 1,000 paces. In Roman times, that was about 5,280 feet—the same as our mile today.

This system of measurement came to us from the ancient tribes of Britain. In the year 1100, the *yard* was added to the list of length measurements. A yard was the length of the king of Britain's arm.

Early Units of Measure

All these measurements had one problem. One man's hand—or foot— was not the same size as another man's. To solve this problem, the British created the *imperial standard yard*. They made a bronze bar and

notched two marks in it to show an exact yard.

Meanwhile, in France, scientists had been working on another measurement system. This was based on the distance between the North Pole and the Equator. The scientists set a meter as one ten-millionth of that distance. They made a metal rod equal to that distance.

Scientists then found new ways to set the meter. In 1960, U.S. mathematicians measured the meter based on the wavelengths of light from a substance called krypton-86. In 1983, the meter was defined again. It became 1/299,792,458 of the length of a path that light travels in a vacuum in a second. That is more reliable because the speed of light does not change.

Adopting the Metric System

Most countries today use the metric system because it is easier to use than the English system. The metric system is based on units of 10. A centimeter is 10 millimeters. A decimeter is 10 centimeters. Officials in the United States have been trying to persuade Americans to switch to the metric system for more than a hundred years.

Unit 1 Review: PACA

> In 1866, Congress made the metric system legal. Today, the metric system is the standard in science and medicine. The sport of track also uses the metric system.
>
> In 1965, Britain gave up its ancient system. In 1971, the U.S. commerce secretary recommended that the United States use the metric system.
>
> Four years later, President Gerald Ford signed the Metric Conversion Act. Since then, the United States has been moving slowly toward joining the rest of the world in using the metric system.

Use your notes and charts to help you answer the questions below.

1. The imperial standard bar was designed
   a. to make the king's arm the standard yard.
   b. so that there was a standard yard measurement.
   c. for use by merchants in Britain.
   d. to make the yard the measure used around the world.

2. The current meter is based on
   a. the speed of light.
   b. the light spectrum.
   c. radiation from krypton-86.
   d. the imperial yard.

3. Many countries use the metric system because
   a. the measurements of the metric system are more precise.
   b. the system of yards is not scientific.
   c. the metric system is easy to use.
   d. people voted to accept it.

4. Summarize how measurement systems have changed since ancient days.

   Today we have more precise methods of measurement. We also follow the metric system—
   the standard in science and medicine.

5. Should the United States ban the use of the English system? Explain.

   Answers will vary but students should use textual information to support their opinions.

Unit *2* Strategy: **DRTA**

Understand It...... DRTA stands for Directed Reading and Thinking Activity. DRTA works well when you can make some predictions about what you will read. When you use DRTA, you preview to see what the author wants to tell you. You look at the headings, subheadings, the topic sentences, and the illustrations. You make predictions about what you will read. Then you read to see if your predictions are correct, and you change your predictions if necessary. In this way, you make sure you understand the evidence that supports the main point of the writing.

Try It............... The article starting on the next page is about the statistical chances that high-school and college athletes have of becoming professional players. Follow along with a student who used the DRTA strategy.

Strategy Tip

Bold type or tables often highlight important information. Look for them as you read.

Step 1. Preview the article and predict what you will read.

When the student picked up the article, he previewed it. He looked at the title, the subheadings, the topic sentences, and the tables. He thought:

This article is about how many high-school and college athletes become professional athletes.

After previewing, the student made some predictions about what he would learn. He wrote them in the Preview box of his DRTA chart. Preview the article and add two of your own predictions to the chart.

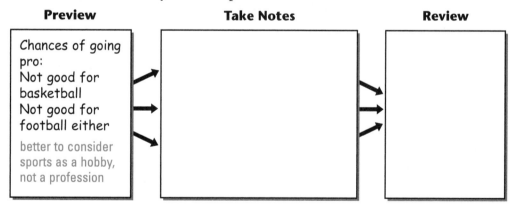

Preview | Take Notes | Review

Chances of going pro:
Not good for basketball
Not good for football either
better to consider sports as a hobby, not a profession

Strategy Tip

Your notes are for you. Any shorthand system you use to make notes will work if *you* understand it.

Step 2. Read, then take notes.

As you read, watch for evidence that supports your predictions. When you are finished reading, write the evidence for your predictions in the Take Notes box. If your predictions are wrong, cross them out. You also might find information that you didn't predict. Write that information, and add the evidence or facts that support it. Here's how the student began thinking about the predictions he made:

I was right. It's about the chances of making a pro team, specifically in basketball and football.

DRTA

Notice the evidence the student wrote. He found evidence to support his prediction and then added it to the Take Notes box. Add your own notes to the chart after you read.

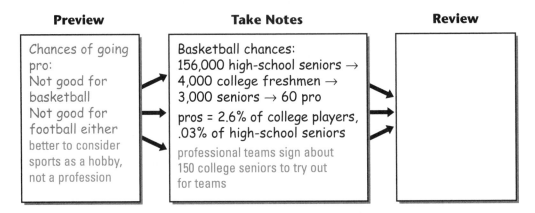

Preview	Take Notes	Review
Chances of going pro: *Not good for basketball* *Not good for football either* *better to consider sports as a hobby, not a profession*	Basketball chances: 156,000 high-school seniors → 4,000 college freshmen → 3,000 seniors → 60 pro pros = 2.6% of college players, .03% of high-school seniors *professional teams sign about 150 college seniors to try out for teams*	

The Chances of Going Pro

Every high-school athlete dreams of playing professional sports. Are such dreams realistic? For some athletes, of course, they are. Michael Jordan did go to high school. Let's say you're a very good—perhaps very, very good—high-school player. Should you stop working on social studies and start working on your jump shot? Read to find out.

Basketball
You may be a very good basketball player. You may even be an unbelievable player. You may be the best player in your high school's history. Right now, about 546,000 other students play high-school basketball too. Of those, about 156,000 are seniors.

Of the high-school players who go to college, about 4,000 will make a team, according to the **NCAA** (National Collegiate Athletic Association). Here is the formula: the percentage of players who go from high-school to college basketball equals the number of college freshmen players divided by the number of high-school senior players times 100.

**% of players who go
from high school to pro basketball =**

college freshmen ÷ h.s. seniors x 100
4,000 freshmen ÷ 156,000 seniors x 100 = 2.6% college players
60 pros ÷ 156,000 h.s. seniors x 100 = .038% NBA pros

As you can see, only about 2.6% of high-school seniors earn a place on a college team.

Vocabulary Tip
The full name of the *NCAA* appears in parentheses after its initials. The next time you see *NCAA*, you probably will not see its full name. Take note of these initials so you'll remember what they stand for.

Now let's say you are a *brilliant* college player. You play NCAA ball all four years. The total number of basketball players on college teams is about 15,000. By the time those players are seniors, about 3,000 remain.

The next hurdle, of course, is making a pro team. Of those 3,000 college seniors, 60 go on to play their rookie year for a pro team. That means that only 2% of college seniors join a pro team. So the chance that any high-school senior will end up joining a pro team is .038%.

Football

Here is the breakdown for future pro football players. More football players sign than basketball players. But in the United States, 958,000 high-school boys play football. That's almost a million. Of those players, 274,000 are seniors.

The NCAA has 54,000 college football players. Of those, 19,000 are freshmen. Here is the formula: the percentage of players who go from high-school to college football equals the number of college freshmen players divided by the number of high-school senior players times 100.

**% of players who go
from high school to pro football =**

college freshmen ÷ h.s. seniors x 100
19,000 freshmen ÷ 274,000 seniors x 100 = 6.9% college players
137 pros ÷ 274,000 h.s. seniors x 100 = 0.05% NFL pros

As you can see, only 6.9% of high-school football players play NCAA football during their freshman year in college. By the time college football players are seniors, only 11,000 players remain.

Professional football teams sign 150 college seniors to try out for their teams. You can calculate the percentage. Divide the number of the seniors signed by the number of college seniors playing. Now multiply that by 100. Only 1.4% of college seniors playing football even get the chance to try out to become pro football players.

If you are a high-school senior playing football, your chance of becoming a professional player is .05%. So keep practicing your game and keep dreaming of making the pros—but keep studying, too.

Step 3. Review what you have read.

Before you put your predictions and notes away, make sure they aren't just on paper. They should be in your mind too. Do you understand what you wrote? Can you close your eyes and think of the main points? Check your understanding by writing a summary of the article. When you summarize, you put the author's thoughts into your own words. This helps you understand and remember your reading.

The student began to write his summary in the Review box. Finish the summary with your own thoughts on the article.

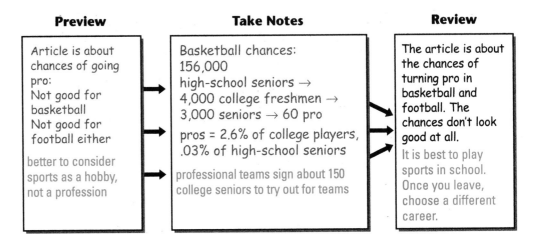

Preview	Take Notes	Review
Article is about chances of going pro: Not good for basketball Not good for football either better to consider sports as a hobby, not a profession	Basketball chances: 156,000 high-school seniors → 4,000 college freshmen → 3,000 seniors → 60 pro pros = 2.6% of college players, .03% of high-school seniors professional teams sign about 150 college seniors to try out for teams	The article is about the chances of turning pro in basketball and football. The chances don't look good at all. It is best to play sports in school. Once you leave, choose a different career.

Apply It. . . . . Use the DRTA strategy with a reading assignment you have. Preview your reading. Look at headings, subheadings, topic sentences, tables, illustrations—anything that might point to a main idea. Make predictions about the topic. Think about your predictions as you read.

When you finish reading, check to see if your predictions were right. Add facts, supporting evidence, and main points, if you missed any. Finally, write a summary of the important points. That will help you remember the information.

You can use your DRTA chart to study later. If you took clear notes and organized your ideas logically in a summary, the chart should be all you need to review.

Lesson 5
Number Sense: The Million-Dollar Minute

Understand It...... Do you watch much television? If you do, you probably see a lot of commercials. Have you ever wondered why commercials constantly interrupt your favorite programs? In this selection, you will discover the answer. DRTA is a good strategy to use here because you already know something about commercials.

Try It............. Start by copying the DRTA chart shown below onto another sheet of paper. Then preview the reading. What does the title mean? How could a minute be worth a million dollars? Make predictions about what type of information the selection will contain. Record your predictions in the Preview box.

Then read the selection. As you read, gather evidence that supports your predictions. Write the evidence in the Take Notes box. Also note any important information you did not predict. Finally, after you finish reading, summarize the selection in the Review box.

Strategy Tip

When you preview, look for repeated words. *Advertising, cost, commercial,* and *network* appear often in this selection. Think about these terms as you make predictions.

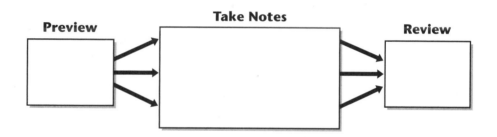

Preview → Take Notes → Review

Vocabulary Tip

Some words have specialized meanings in particular fields. How does the meaning of *product* here differ from other meanings of *product*?

The Million-Dollar Minute

Many Americans spend a great deal of their free time watching television. On average, Americans watch about seven hours of television *each day*! Only people in Japan watch more TV. Studies show that Japanese viewers spend more than nine hours a day in front of a television.

Commercials make up a large percentage of that viewing time. In the United States, people watch advertising for more than 13 minutes of every television hour. In Ireland, fewer than five minutes of every television hour is used for commercials. The number drops rapidly in Japan and France. People in those countries spend less than one minute of every television hour watching commercials.

Why do commercials take up so much airtime? The answer is money. Television networks charge for commercial time. Companies pay the networks huge sums of money to advertise their **products**. The networks use the money to pay for programs.

Number Sense:
The Million-Dollar Minute

Strategy Tip

In math texts, information in charts can help you understand the topic. Note this information in your DRTA chart.

The amount charged for time to show commercials varies. Shows with large audiences have high ratings. Ratings refer to the number of television sets in the United States that are tuned in to a program.

Networks use ratings to set fees for commercial costs. The prices are measured in "cost per thousand TV viewers," or **CPM**. (*M* is the Roman-numeral abbreviation for "thousand.") For example, suppose the CPM of a program is $30 per minute. Ratings show that the program has an average audience of one million viewers. A one-minute commercial would cost $30,000. If ratings showed that two million viewers usually watch the program, a one-minute commercial would cost $60,000.

Vocabulary Tip

The initials *CPM* are an abbreviation of an important term, "cost per thousand TV viewers." Note the term in your DRTA chart.

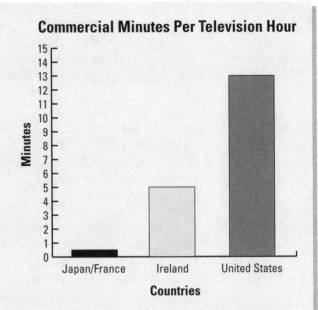

Commercial Minutes Per Television Hour

A commercial shown during a hit program can cost as much as $1 million. One-time programs with high ratings, such as the Super Bowl, can command more than $1 million for a 30-second commercial. Commercial airtime for the series-ending episode of *Seinfeld* was rumored to cost between $1.4 and $1.8 million for a 30-second ad.

So the next time your favorite program is interrupted by a commercial, don't grumble. Think about why someone would pay so much to get your attention.

When you finish taking notes, look over your DRTA chart. Use it to summarize the main points of the selection in the Review box.

Apply It. . . . . To check your understanding of the selection, circle the best answer to each question below.

1. Which choice arranges these countries in order from the least percentage of a television hour used for commercials to the greatest percentage?
   a. Ireland, France, Japan
   b. Japan, Ireland, United States
   c. United States, France, Ireland
   d. Ireland, Japan, United States

2. Networks devote almost 25 percent of television time to commercials
   a. to obtain money from advertisers.
   b. to help viewers become informed customers.
   c. to help viewers compare different products.
   d. to allow advertisers to test their products.

3. Which statement below describes how ratings affect fees for commercial airtime?
   a. the lower the ratings, the higher the fee
   b. the higher the ratings, the higher the fee
   c. the lower the fee, the higher the ratings
   d. no relationship between ratings and fees

Test Tip

When you *infer*, you think about what you know. Then you use the information to make a new statement. To answer question 4, think about how the fee for commercial airtime is calculated. Also think about how often the Super Bowl occurs.

4. What can you infer from the fee charged for a commercial aired during the Super Bowl?
   a. Few shoppers watch the Super Bowl.
   b. People who enjoy football are considered good shoppers.
   c. The Super Bowl has a low CPM.
   d. The Super Bowl has extremely high ratings.

5. Suppose the cost of a certain one-minute commercial was $5,000. What does that mean?
   a. The commercial aired during a program with high ratings.
   b. The commercial aired during a program with average ratings.
   c. The commercial aired during a program with low ratings.
   d. The commercial advertised a poor product.

Use the lines below to write your answers for numbers 6 and 7. Use your DRTA chart to help you.

6. Write a paragraph for a grade-school newspaper that explains why so many commercials appear on television.

   Students might focus on why companies make commercials, who watches these
   commercials, and how commercials affect the consumers.

   _____

   _____

7. Suppose you have designed a new type of CD player. You decide to advertise your product on television. Name three programs during which you want your commercial to air. Give reasons for your choices.

   Students may choose to air their commercial during programs watched by a very
   large audience, which may include sporting events, sit-coms, or talk shows. They
   should explain why they chose the programs and why the audience for the shows
   might buy their CD player.

   _____

Real-life Math: Playing the Market

Lesson 6

Understand It...... If you have ever watched the news on TV, you have heard about the stock market. You might have heard your parents talking about stocks. The DRTA strategy can help you understand this selection. When you have finished reading, you will know more about buying and selling stock.

Try It.............. Copy the DRTA chart shown below on another sheet of paper. Then preview the selection. Look at the subheadings, the first and last sentences of each paragraph, and the topic sentences. Write your predictions in the Preview box.

Next, read the selection. Look for evidence that supports your predictions. Write this evidence and any other important information you find in the Take Notes box. If your predictions are wrong, cross them off and write the points you did not predict. When you have finished reading, you will summarize the selection in the Review box.

Strategy Tip

When you preview, look for repeated words. The terms *stock market, stock, share,* and *broker* appear often in this selection. Use these terms to make some predictions about what you will read.

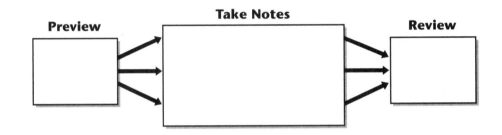

Playing the Market

During the Revolutionary War, colonial banks began to sell parts of their business to people. They did this to raise money to fight Great Britain. People gave the banks a certain amount of money. The banks gave each purchaser a piece of paper to show that the person owned part of the bank. That was the beginning of the stock market.

After the war ended, some New York businessmen signed an agreement. They agreed to buy and sell parts of companies for other people. They would charge buyers a fee for the service. The men set up offices at 40 Wall Street in New York City. The building became the New York Stock Exchange. The New York Stock Exchange is still in New York City. At the Exchange, people buy and sell stocks every day.

Anyone can buy stock in a company. A buyer must first decide which company to invest money in. Then the buyer contacts a broker. A broker is a person who buys and sells stocks for others. The broker tells the buyer the value of one **share** of stock. A single share might have a

Vocabulary Tip

The word *share* has a variety of meanings. Compare how a group of brokers and a group of young children might use the word.

value of 10 1/2 points. That means that the buyer must pay $10.50 to own one part of the company. The buyer usually buys more than a single share. The cost of the purchase is calculated by multiplying the total number of shares by the cost of a single share.

The buyer must also pay the broker a fee for making the sale. Some fees are a percentage of the total sale. Other fees are a constant amount, such as $100. The broker's fee is called a **commission**.

The value of a company's shares changes many times a day. Sometimes, the value goes up. This means that a single share is worth more money than the buyer paid. At other times, the value goes down. This means that a single share is worth less money than the buyer paid.

People who own stocks want to know how much their shares are worth. Most major newspapers print that information in the business section. The value of each stock sold at the stock exchange is listed. Shareholders can find out whether they have lost money or made money on their stocks.

Because the value of a share changes, playing the stock market involves risk. In the table below, you'll see how the changes in share prices affected shareholders in José's National Appliance Center. Suppose a buyer paid $10.50 per share. Then the value of the stock dropped 2 3/4 points. This means the stock's value decreased by $2.75. The new value was only 7 3/4 points or $7.75. The shareholder lost $2.75 per share.

In the second row of the table, you'll see what happened next. The same stock went up 5 1/2 points. The value increased by $5.50 per share. The new value was 13 1/4 points, or $13.25 per share. The shareholder made back the money that he or she lost, plus an extra $2.75 per share.

Vocabulary Tip

In textbooks, definitions often appear *after* the new word. In this paragraph, the definition of *commission* appears *before* the term.

Strategy Tip

Tables are often used in math textbooks to highlight important information. This table illustrates what the text tells you about how prices can go up or down on the stock market.

José's National Appliance Center

Yesterday's Stock Value	↑↓	New Stock Value
$10.50 per share	down 2 $\frac{3}{4}$ or $2.75	$10.50 – $2.75 = $7.75
$7.75 per share	up 5 $\frac{1}{2}$ or $5.50	$7.75 + $5.50 = $13.25

Millions of people own stocks. Each day, billions of dollars worth of stocks are traded on the New York Stock Exchange. Some people make money. Some people lose money. However, every shareholder can be called an "owner of a company."

Real-life Math:
Playing the Market

Now complete your DRTA chart. Write a summary of what you learned in the Review box.

Apply It. . . . . To check your understanding of the selection, circle the best answer to each question below.

1. A broker is a
    a. person who works at a bank.
    b. person who owns part of a company.
    (c.) person who buys and sells stocks for others.
    d. person who works in New York City.

2. A share of stock with a value of 7 1/2 points is worth
    a. $7.34.
    b. $73.40.
    c. $7.75.
    (d.) $7.50.

3. A commission is a fee
    (a.) charged by a broker for buying or selling stocks.
    b. charged by the company selling its stock.
    c. charged to enter the New York Stock Exchange.
    d. charged by a bank to purchase part of its company.

4. If a stock drops 2 points, then
    a. a broker has bought two shares of the stock.
    b. the new value of a single share is $2.00 more than the previous value.
    (c.) the new value of a single share is $2.00 less than the previous value.
    d. the commission for buying a share of the stock is $2.00.

Test Tip

A conclusion is a judgment or decision reached after careful thought. What judgment can you make after thinking about the main points of the selection?

5. What conclusion can you reach after reading the selection?
    a. Only serious businessmen can buy stocks.
    (b.) Shareholders do not know whether they will make or lose money.
    c. Buying stocks is a sure way to earn money.
    d. Bank stocks are good investments.

Use the lines below to write your answers for numbers 6 and 7. Use your DRTA chart to help you.

6. You've decided to buy stock in a company. What would you do next?

    Students should note that after deciding which stock to buy, they need to consider the broker fee, the current and long-term value of the stock, the risk, and how many stocks to buy.

7. Suppose you were given $1,000. You can either put the money in the bank or the stock market. What would you do? Explain your decision.

    Students might choose to put their money in a bank, where there is little risk. They might also choose to invest their money in the stock market, where there may be high risk but a greater chance of making more money.

Lesson 7
Statistics: Nielsen Ratings

Understand It...... What's your favorite television show? If you ask ten people that question, you'll probably get ten different answers. The answers are very important to the networks that broadcast shows and to the advertisers who buy airtime for their commercials. In this reading, you'll find out why.

Try It.............. Because you probably know enough about TV to make some predictions, the DRTA strategy could be a good choice with this reading. Copy the DRTA chart onto a sheet of paper. Then preview the reading. Make predictions about the kind of information you will learn.

After recording your predictions in the Preview box, read the selection. Gather evidence that backs up your predictions and other important information. Write the evidence in the Take Notes column of the chart. After you read, write a summary of the reading in the Review box.

Strategy Tip

When you preview the selection, look for words that are repeated. *Nielsen Media Research, viewers, meters*, and *ratings* appear often. Focus on these terms as you make your predictions.

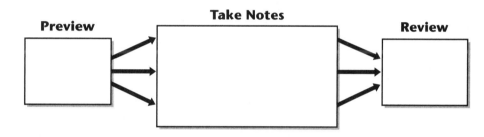

Preview | Take Notes | Review

Vocabulary Tip

The word *viewership* might not be familiar, but you probably know the word *viewer*. Reading the paragraph carefully will tell you that *viewership* is another word for *"audience."*

Nielsen Ratings

Your family probably has one thing in common with most American families. The television set is on for some part of every day. In the United States, approximately 99 million households have at least one TV. Each person who watches TV is a possible consumer, or buyer, of a product. Advertisers know that television commercials are one way to reach consumers. They spend almost $40 billion each year on TV ads.

Advertisers want to make sure they spend their money wisely. Therefore, they want to know how many and what kind of people will watch their commercials. So, how do advertisers get that vital information? The Nielsen ratings provide it.

Nielsen Media Research produces the Nielsen ratings. It uses meters to track **viewership**. The company chooses television households at random. If a household agrees to participate, the company places a meter on each TV that notes the program or channel, the time the TV is on, and the number of times the channel changes. The company also collects information about a show's general **audience**. Information about each viewer is collected when he or she presses an identification button.

Statistics:
Nielsen Ratings

In the middle of each night, the company collects information from all the meters. The data is processed, and by noon the following day, networks and advertisers have the ratings. A high Nielsen rating means a large number of households tuned in.

Rating and Market Share

There are two main kinds of information that comprise the Nielsen ratings—the ratings and the share. The *rating* is how many households in the United States were tuned in to a particular show. Often the rating numbers are followed by the share. The share is the percentage of television sets that are on and tuned to a show. Here is how both of these numbers are determined.

The United States has about 99 million households that own TV sets. A 10 rating means that 10 percent of those, or about 9.9 million, were tuned to the show. To determine the rating of a show, you would use this equation:

$$\text{rating} = \frac{\text{households tuned to a show}}{\text{total households with TV sets}} \times 100 \text{ points}$$

The *share* of a show is a comparison between that show and the others on TV at the same time. For example, if a show had a 20 share, 20 percent of the people with their sets on had the sets tuned to that show. Here is how to determine a show's share:

$$\text{share} = \frac{\text{households tuned to a particular show}}{\text{total households with TV sets on}} \times 100 \text{ points}$$

The Cost of Advertising

Once networks have the ratings, they can determine the cost per thousand viewers, or CPM. (*M* is the Roman-numeral sign for "thousand.") Networks look at the ratings to see how popular the show is. They look at the **demographics**, or age, sex, and location of the viewers. The more desirable the demographics are, the more the network can charge for advertising time. For example, younger viewers aged 18 to 24 years old are popular targets for many advertisers. The shows that attract these viewers may have a higher CPM. The CPM for a show might be $4 a minute. If its audience is 2 million viewers, a 60-second commercial would be $8,000. For popular shows, rates can reach $1 million for a minute of commercial time.

For special broadcasts like the Superbowl, some advertisers will pay large sums of money. In 1999, the price for a thirty-second commercial during the Superbowl was $1.6 million dollars. At those rates, the CPM is very high. It's the huge number of viewers for such once-a-year events that advertisers are after, and not a reasonable cost per viewer.

Strategy Tip

What do these two equations tell you about the Nielsen ratings? Add this information to your DRTA chart.

Vocabulary Tip

Look around the word *demographics* for context clues that can help you understand its meaning. For example, an author can place a definition between commas.

The ratings and shares that network television shows earn today are much lower than they were two decades ago. Back then, there were only three networks. If a show had a 30 share, that meant one-third of the people with their TV sets on were watching that show. A 30 share was about average when there were only three choices.

Today, though, there are often 40 or more channels viewers can choose from. If every channel had an equal share, they would each have less than a 3 share. So, in today's TV market, a 30 share is extremely rare. Viewers have many more choices and advertisers have to look at demographics and CPMs more closely.

When you've completed your DRTA chart, look over your notes. Write a few sentences that summarize the main points in the Review section of your chart.

Apply It . . . . To check your understanding of the selection, circle the best answer to each question below.

1. About how much money do advertisers spend each year on television commercials?
   a. $4 million
   b. $40 million
   c. $40 billion
   d. $400 billion

2. How does Nielsen Media Research gather information about television viewership?
   a. from interviews
   b. through meters
   c. through written surveys sent to every household
   d. from telephone surveys

3. Nielsen Media Research collects information about all of the following *except*
   a. the number of times the station was changed.
   b. the age of a television viewer.
   c. the number of hours a television set is turned on daily.
   d. the price of a television set.

4. The word *share* as used in the section "Rating and Market Share" means
   a. the percentage of people in the United States watching TV.
   b. the percentage of households with TV sets on watching one particular show.
   c. the number of people with TVs who are watching a show.
   d. the number of households who are watching TV.

Test Tip

To find the correct answer to question 4, carefully read each choice. A single word can make an answer wrong or right in a multiple-choice question.

Statistics:
Nielsen Ratings

5. An advertiser would be willing to spend a higher CPM for a show because
   a. it is a show about the product being advertised.
   b. the share is low and the audience is expected to be large.
   c. the show appeals to a demographic the advertiser wants to target.
   d. both a and b

Use the lines below to write your answers for numbers 6 and 7. Use your DRTA chart to help you.

6. List three products that are advertised during TV shows that you watch. Describe the audience of the shows.

   Lists will vary but might include personal-care products, clothing companies,
   fast-food restaurants, and beverages. Descriptions might include teenagers who
   are interested in how they look.

7. If the CPM for a show is $8 a minute and it has 7 million viewers, how much would a 60-second commercial cost? Describe how you found your answer.

   $8 per minute x 7 million viewers ÷ 1,000 = $56,000 for a 60-second commercial

Lesson 8

Problem Solving: Mental Math

Understand It...... You make mathematical calculations in your head every day. You look at your change and decide if you have enough to buy a soda. You estimate what the tip on a meal will be. In this selection, you will learn to make different kinds of calculations in your head.

Try It............. DRTA is a good reading strategy to use with this selection because you probably know something about mental math. Copy the DRTA chart below onto a sheet of paper. Then preview the reading. Write predictions in the chart about the kind of information it contains.

After recording your predictions in the chart, read the selection. Look for information that supports your predictions. Write this information in the Take Notes column. Then summarize the selection in the Review column.

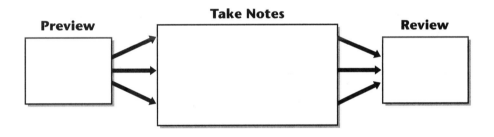

Preview   **Take Notes**   **Review**

Vocabulary Tip

The word *round* has a meaning in math that is different from its meaning in other subjects. When you round a number in math, you make a number larger or smaller so you can work with it more easily.

Mental Math

Figuring out problems in your head, or using mental math, is a very handy skill. How often have you used a piece of paper and a pencil to figure out the answer to a problem? With some new methods, you will be able to use mental math.

Working with Round Numbers

When you **round** a number, you go up or down to a number that is easier to use. Let's say you wanted to add 497 and 354. Those numbers look difficult to add in your head, but the operation becomes easier when you round them. Here's how to do it:

Step 1: Round the numbers, remembering what you added or subtracted. For example, rewrite the numbers above:

497 = (500–3)

354 = (350+4)

Problem Solving:
Mental Math

Strategy Tip

When you are reading math that contains steps or an equation, review by creating a problem and then solving it. That will show if you understand the process.

Vocabulary Tip

In math textbooks, you will often see terms explained with both a definition and examples. What does *place value* mean?

Step 2: Add the rounded numbers.

```
 500
+350
 850
```

Step 3: To find the exact answer, add or subtract the numbers left over after rounding.

```
4–3 = 1
850        497
+   1      +354
851        851
```

The same technique works for subtraction, as well. You subtract your rounded numbers, and then add or subtract the leftover numbers.

Adding by Place Value

If you need to add or subtract larger numbers, you can add or subtract by working with **place value**, or ones, tens, hundreds, and so on. For example, imagine you have to add 526 and 493. Here's how you can break down those numbers.

Step 1: Add the largest place value, or the hundreds, together.

```
 500
+400
 900
```

Step 2: Add the next largest place value. In this case, add the tens together.

```
 20
+90
110
```

Step 3: Add the next largest grouping. In this case, add the ones.

```
 6
+3
 9
```

Step 4: Add the numbers from each operation for the total.

```
 900
 110
+   9
1,019 Total
```

Multiplying the Pieces

When you need to multiply large numbers, you can break the numbers into smaller figures that are easier to work with. Follow these steps.

Step 1: Suppose you are multiplying 23 X 17. First, make one number smaller so you can multiply in your head. In this case, you would break 23 into 20 + 3.

Step 2: Now, multiply the second number by each of the numbers you broke down.

Multiply 20 by 17   20 X 17 = 340

Multiply   3 by 17   3 X 17 =   51

Step 3: To get the final answer, add those two numbers. Check your answer by using paper and pencil to multiply the original numbers.

```
 340   Check:  23
+ 51          x17
 391          161
             +23
             391
```

Try these techniques next time you need to do math in your head. Remember that you can use these methods with money, units, or any kinds of numbers.

Look over your DRTA notes. Did you include all the important parts you learned about mental math? Write a few sentences that summarize the selection in the Review box of your chart.

Apply It . . . . To check your understanding of the selection, circle the best answer to each question below.

Test Tip

Question 1 tests your ability to sequence the steps in a process. The words *immediately before* show that you must name the last thing to do before you add the extra numbers.

1. When you add by rounding numbers, what should you do after you rewrite the numbers?
   a. Add the rounded numbers.
   b. Subtract the rounded numbers.
   c. Round the numbers.
   d. Read the problem.

2. If you are adding 289 to 876 by using place value, what would you do first?
   a. Set up an equation.
   b. Subtract 200 from 800.
   c. Add 80 to 70.
   d. Add 200 and 800.

Problem Solving:
Mental Math

3. "If you need to add or subtract larger numbers, you can add or subtract by working with place value, or the parts of the numbers—ones, tens, hundreds, and so on." In that sentence, *place value* means
   a. whether the numbers are 100s, 10s, or 1s.
   b. larger or smaller than 10.
   c. equal to another number.
   d. none of the above

4. What do these mental math calculations have in common?
   a. They all deal with subtraction and addition.
   b. They all deal with addition and multiplication.
   c. They all work with numbers that are easier to use.
   d. They all need a calculator.

5. What is the main idea of this selection?
   a. You can solve any simple equation with pencil and paper.
   b. Following a plan can only help you answer problems that have large numbers.
   c. You can solve math problems without pencil and paper.
   d. The same plan can be used to solve any kind of math problem.

Use the lines below to write your answers for numbers 6 and 7. Use your DRTA chart to help you.

6. Describe a situation in which you would use one of these mental math methods.

   Sample answer: When making a purchase, you might round off the cost of each
   item to get an idea of the total cost. This will allow you to see if you have enough
   money to make the purchase.

7. Write an explanation for how you would multiply 35 by 18 using mental math.

   Step 1: Break down the larger number into 30 and 5; Step 2: Multiply 30 x 18 =
   540; multiply 5 x 18 = 90; Step 3: Add the two numbers 540 + 90 = 630.

Unit 2 Review: **DRTA**

In this unit, you have practiced using the DRTA reading strategy. Use this strategy when you read the selection below. Use a separate sheet of paper to draw a chart, take notes, and summarize what you learn.

Hint *Remember that all reading strategies have activities for before, during, and after reading. To review these steps, look at the inside back cover of this book.*

Figuring Miles Per Gallon

On every new car is a sticker that explains how many miles the car gets to a gallon of gas. That number is called the car's *mileage*. The more miles to a gallon of gas the car gets, the less the car costs to run.

Suppose you are buying a used car that gets only 6 miles to the gallon. You will spend a lot of money on gas.

You can easily check the miles per gallon that your car gets. First, though, you need to know some terms. One of these is **mpg**. That stands for *miles per gallon*. Another term is **odometer**. That is the equipment on the car's dashboard that shows how many miles you have driven the car.

To calculate mpg, use these steps:

Step 1 When you stop for gas, fill the tank up completely. Write down the reading on the odometer.

Step 2 The next time you buy gas again, fill the tank completely. Then write down the odometer reading. Also write down the number of gallons you needed to fill the tank.

Step 3 Find out how many miles you drove from the first odometer reading to the second. Subtract your old odometer reading from your new odometer reading.

Step 4 Divide the number of miles you drove by the number of gallons of gas needed to fill your tank. That number is your mpg.

Here is the formula:

Mpg = new odometer reading – old odometer reading ÷ gallons of gas needed to fill the tank

Let's say you filled your tank in one city. Your odometer read 3,876. You travel to another city. Your odometer now reads 4,071. You fill your tank with 13 gallons of gas. To figure out how many miles you are getting per gallon, you would do the following calculations:

1. Subtract the first odometer reading from the second to find out how many miles you traveled.

$4071 - 3876 = 195$

You have traveled 195 miles.

Unit 2 Review: DRTA

2. Divide 195 by the number of gallons of gas you used. That number is 13.

$195 \div 13 = 15$

Your car gets 15 miles to a gallon of gas, or 15 mpg.

The formula looks like this:

$(4071 - 3876) \div 13 =$
$195 \div 13 = 15$

Knowing how to find mpg is a useful skill. It can tell you exactly how much your car costs to run.

Use your notes and charts to help you answer the questions below.

1. What is an odometer?
   a. a device that determines miles per gallon
   b. the way you calculate miles per gallon
   (c.) a device that shows how many miles you have driven
   d. the number of miles you have driven a car

2. Knowing your mpg can be useful if
   a. you want to know how fast you are going.
   b. you want to know how much gas you have left.
   (c.) you want to know how expensive your car is to run.
   d. you want to see if a car is too expensive to buy.

3. To calculate mpg, after you know how many miles you have driven since you last filled your gas tank, you first
   a. subtract the number of miles you have driven from the first odometer reading.
   b. convert to mpg.
   c. divide that number by the number of miles you have traveled to find mpg.
   (d.) divide that number by the number of gallons of gas you used.

4. Suppose your odometer reads 7544 miles when you fill your car with gas. The next time you fill your gas tank your odometer reads 7765. Your tank takes 13 gallons of gas. How many miles per gallon (mpg) does your car get?

   Answers should demonstrate an understanding of the steps outlined in the selection.
   7765−7544= 221; 221÷13=17. Following the steps will prove that the car gets 17 miles per gallon.

5. Suppose you are selling your car and it has an mpg reading of 27. Explain to a buyer why this is important.

   This will tell a buyer that the car is inexpensive to run because it gets so many miles (27) per gallon.

Unit 3 Strategy: **KWL Plus**

KWL Plus

Understand It......

Active readers always approach reading with a strategy. They think about what they will be reading. They have an idea of why they are reading. After they read, they figure out whether they understand what they have read. KWL Plus (**K**now, **W**ant to Know, **L**earned) is one way of putting all those ideas to work for you. The "Plus" part on the strategy helps you put these pieces together by summarizing what you've learned.

Try It..............

The essay on pages 46–48 presents different opinions about the salaries of professional athletes. Follow along with a student who used the KWL Plus strategy.

Step 1. Write what you already know about the topic.

Strategy Tip

Think about what you might have already read or heard about the topic as you fill out the K section. You might have heard, read, or talked about athletes' salaries with friends.

When you think about what you already know, you focus your mind on what you will be reading. When you see new information, you will be able to connect it to what you know. After you think about the topic, preview the essay. Here's what the student thought as he considered the topic and then previewed the essay.

People on TV are always talking about the high salaries made by pro athletes. I remember reading something about how high Michael Jordan's salary was. This will probably be about whether players should be paid that much.

Look at what the student wrote in the K section of his KWL chart. Then add at least two things you know to the list.

K (What I know)	W (What I want to know)	L (What I've learned)
Some pro athletes earn high salaries. Most athletes earn more than other professionals, such as teachers. Some athletes will not sign contracts unless their demands for high salaries are met.		

Step 2. Write what you want to know.

Strategy Tip

Make sure that some of your questions begin with *how* and *why*.

In the next section, you write questions that will help you focus your thinking as you read. Here is what the student thought:

I want to know what the arguments are for and against high salaries.

In the W section, the student listed two questions he wanted to answer. Add at least two things you want to learn as you read this selection.

KWL Plus

K (What I know)	W (What I want to know)	L (What I've learned)
Some pro athletes earn high salaries. Most athletes earn more than other professionals, such as teachers. Some athletes will not sign contracts unless their demands for high salaries are met.	Why are people against high salaries? Why do athletes earn such high salaries now? Are ticket prices higher because of the higher salaries?	

Step 3. Write what you learn.

After you read the essay, write the important points in the L section of the KWL chart. Watch for information that answers your questions. You may learn important information that you did not ask questions about. Write notes about that information in the L column too. The student reading this article already wrote one main point that answers his first question.

K (What I know)	W (What I want to know)	L (What I've learned)
Some pro athletes earn high salaries. Most athletes earn more than other professionals, such as teachers. Some athletes will not sign contracts unless their demands for high salaries are met.	Why are people against high salaries? Why do athletes earn such high salaries now? Are ticket prices higher because of the higher salaries?	Against high salaries: Athletes aren't helping the world, so they don't deserve high salaries. Against: Young athletes may feel that they don't need to complete their education because they will make high salaries.

For: The athletes are the ones who generate the revenue so they deserve the salaries.

Strategy Tip
Thinking about why you are reading helps you focus your reading.

Strategy Tip
Notice that the section headings signal different opinions about the topic.

Debate: Are Pro Athletes' Salaries out of Control?

Should a basketball player earn more money for playing three minutes in a professional basketball game than a teacher makes in an entire year? Raise the topic of professional athletes' salaries in any group of people. Everyone has an opinion about this explosive issue. The following arguments include some, but certainly not all, of those opinions.

These Salaries Are Ridiculous!

It's easy to find people who get worked up about the kind of money athletes make. Statistics such as the one in the first paragraph horrify critics. Think about the kind of money athletes make compared to what most people earn. For example, during his top-earning pro basketball years, Michael Jordan made $71,600 a night while he slept! Playing basketball does nothing to help the world. Basketball doesn't build houses for poor people or even feed them. Michael Jordan earned an absurd amount of money for playing a game!

Do you believe that professional athletes deserve their salaries?

Vocabulary Tip

Sometimes words you know are combined to make a phrase you might not know. If you look at the words *salary cap*, you'll see that the phrase is defined in the next part of the sentence.

Part of what makes NBA salaries absurd is the Larry Bird exception. Larry Bird was a very good NBA player. He negotiated an exception to the NBA's **salary cap**, which said that teams cannot spend more than $35 million a year for the salaries of all their players. The terms of this agreement changed in 1999. The 1999 agreement stated that players will be paid based on their number of years in the NBA. Players with 0–6 years of experience can make up to $9 million per year. Players with 7–9 years can earn up to $11 million per year. Those with 11 or more years can earn $14 million per year.

Out-of-control salaries have helped create the "big baby syndrome" among professional athletes. Many professional athletes are pampered and flattered and admired. They soon get the idea they are different from "ordinary" people. They don't have to play by the rules that the rest of us play by. They earn enormous amounts of money and can buy their way out of trouble. Some professional athletes never grow up. They don't have to because they can pay someone else to handle their responsibilities.

Professional athletes make poor role models. Younger athletes look at the lives the pros lead and want to be like them. "If those guys can make so much money playing ball," young athletes reason, "so can I!" As a result, thousands of young men neglect their education. Dreams of immense wealth lead young people to base their future on unrealistic expectations. They often find themselves unprepared to do anything when they fail to make the cut.

What kind of message do sky-high salaries for athletes send about what is important? The comparison between a teacher's pay and a professional athlete's might be obvious. It's also accurate. What does that tell us about our society? What should we conclude when people who contribute to society can barely feed their families, but those who handle a ball well are millionaires?

Professional Players Are Worth What They Get

Plenty of people believe that professional athletes deserve every penny they get. Who else, they argue, provides so much entertainment

KWL Plus

Vocabulary Tip

Look for clues for the meaning of *revenue* in this paragraph. Athletes create enormous amounts of it. What does *revenue* mean?

Vocabulary Tip

You may know that the word *prospered* means "to have benefited." In this sentence, *prospered* means our country has benefited from a free-market system.

to others? A great team can make a community proud, and that's worth just about any amount of money.

Why don't people who do worthy work earn as much money as professional athletes? That's simple. Those people don't create as much **revenue** for their employers. Athletes create enormous amounts of revenue, so the owners can justify the players' salaries. Should all that money go right into the pockets of the owners? Of course not! It should go to the players, who provide what people pay to watch.

Athletes, of course, understand the way our world works. People often judge a person's worth by the money he or she makes. Athletes want big money not just for its own sake but also for the sense of self-worth it gives them. The size of the salary shows what an athlete is worth compared to other players.

Professional athletes' salaries reflect our economic system. Our country has **prospered** because it is a free-market system. People who provide something the market wants can charge whatever people will pay for it. If something costs $50 million and someone will pay that price, that's what the "something" is worth. That's what happens in a free market. That's the American way—the way that has given us an economy and a society that have flourished. There is no reason to condemn those who have done nothing more than make the system work for them.

4. Use the KWL chart to summarize what you have learned.

When you write a summary, you make a quick check of what you read. Do the main points stay with you? Can you point to the important arguments in what you read?

Here's how the student began his summary. Use this beginning as a model to write your own summary on another sheet of paper.

This essay states the arguments for and against high salaries for professional athletes . . .

Apply It. . . . . Try the KWL Plus strategy on a reading assignment you have. First, draw a KWL chart on another sheet of paper. Identify the topic and then fill in the K section with what you already know about it. Preview the reading, then fill in the W section with what you want to learn from your reading. After you read, fill in the L section. Then use your completed KWL chart to help you write a summary of your reading.

Lesson 9

Calculating Batting Averages: Average Achievement

Understand It...... Have you ever watched a baseball game? Maybe you play baseball. If so, you know that the goal of every batter is to make a hit. Most teams keep track of the number of hits each player makes. This information is used to compute the player's batting average.

In this selection, you will learn about figuring out batting averages. Because you might know some facts about batting averages, the KWL Plus strategy is a good strategy to use to help you understand the selection.

Try It.............. Draw a KWL chart like the one shown below on a separate sheet of paper. Begin by listing everything you know about batting averages in the K column. In the W column, write what you want to know about how batting averages are calculated. Think about these questions as you read the selection. When you've finished reading, you'll write the answers in the L column of your chart. Then you'll practice calculating averages.

Strategy Tip

Include what you know about how to figure out other kinds of averages in the K column of your KWL chart.

K (What I know)	W (What I want to know)	L (What I've learned)

Vocabulary Tip

When you *calculate*, you perform a mathematical operation such as addition or subtraction. How is the word *calculator* related to *calculate*?

Average Achievement

How many different kinds of averages can you think of? There are bowling averages, video game averages, and salary averages. People work an average number of hours per week. They spend an average number of hours watching TV. You have a grade-point average and sleep an average number of hours per night. You probably help with chores at home an average number of hours per week.

People figure out averages to measure overall performance. You might have **calculated** your test average. Your average gave you an idea of your overall grade. That information was useful to you. If your average was lower than you expected, you probably put in extra time studying for the next test.

Sometimes people calculate averages so they can rank things. Bowling averages might be used to rank the members of a bowling team. This information could be used to determine the order in which the team members bowl.

Calculating Batting Averages:
Average Achievement

Strategy Tip

You might want to copy the figures for Belle's and McGwire's batting averages into your KWL chart. You can use them to answer a question about batting averages.

Baseball averages are important, too. Managers usually calculate their hitters' batting averages. A batting average is the ratio of the number of hits a player gets divided by the number of times the player bats. The more hits a player gets, the higher his average is. Fewer hits per number of times at bat means a lower average.

For example, in 1995 Albert Belle went to the plate 546 times. He got a base hit 173 times. What was Belle's batting average for 1995? Divide the number of hits (173) by the number of at-bats (546). This is the ratio of the number of hits to the number of times at bat. The result is .317, which was Belle's batting average.

Three years later, Belle got 200 hits. During the 1998 season, he batted 609 times. What was Belle's batting average that year? If you divide 200 by 609, you find that his average was .328. Belle's average rose.

In that same year, Mark McGwire broke a historic record. He toppled Roger Maris's record for the most home runs hit during a regular season. McGwire hit nine more than Maris did, ending the season with 70 home runs.

You might think that this many home runs would boost McGwire's batting average. In fact, his average for the season was only .299. That's because a home run counts the same as a single when calculating a batting average. McGwire had 152 hits—70 were home runs—in his 509 times at bat. Dividing 152 by 509 yields his batting average of .299.

Albert Belle

Mark McGwire

Now that you have finished reading about figuring out averages, go back and complete the L column of your KWL chart with the information you learned. Be sure you can answer every question listed in the W column.

Instead of writing a summary, practice your averaging skills by calculating the batting averages of your school's or your favorite team's baseball players. If you'd prefer, you can average the number of points per game for basketball players or the number of goals the soccer team scored during the season.

Apply It........... To check your understanding of the selection, circle the best answer to each question below.

1. Why do people calculate averages?
   a. to get an idea of overall performance
   b. to rank things
   c. to practice math skills
   d. both a and b

Test Tip

The author's purpose is the reason he or she wrote the selection. Did you learn something? Did the selection cause you to take a certain stand? Did the selection make you wonder about something?

2. What is the author's purpose for writing this selection?
   a. to inform
   b. to persuade
   c. to ask a question
   d. both a and b

3. What is a batting average?
   a. the number of home runs a player hits per times at bat
   b. the number of walks a player draws plus the number of hits the player gets
   c. the number of hits a player gets per times at bat
   d. the number of times a player strikes out divided by the number of home runs

4. What information is needed to calculate a batting average?
   a. number of times at bat and number of home runs
   b. number of hits and number of times at bat
   c. number of at bats and number of strikeouts
   d. number of walks and number of hits

5. Which mathematical operation is used to figure out a batting average?
   a. division
   b. subtraction
   c. addition
   d. multiplication

Calculating Batting Averages:
Average Achievement

Use the lines below to write your answers for numbers 6 and 7. You can use your KWL chart to help you.

6. During the regular 1998 baseball season, Bernie Williams of the New York Yankees had 169 hits in 499 times at bat. Explain how to calculate his batting average.

    Divide 169 hits by 499 at bats to yield a batting average of .339.

    _____

    _____

    _____

    _____

7. Describe a real-life situation in which finding an average would be helpful to you.

    Students may suggest that it would be helpful to know the average amount of time it takes them to walk to school or the amount of money they spend each week on lunch.

    _____

    _____

    _____

    _____

Lesson 10

Computer Science: Donna Auguste, American Dreamer

Understand It...... This reading profiles a computer designer named Donna Auguste. As an African American female, Donna had to work hard to accomplish her goals. She had to overcome many biases. In this selection, you will read about her life and accomplishments.

Try It.............. The KWL Plus strategy will help you understand the selection. Begin by listing everything you know about computers in the K column. Think about size, weight, what happens when you drop one, how easy or difficult they are to use, what they need to run, and what people do with them. Also consider what you already know about Donna Auguste. The photograph on the next page will give you some information about her.

In the W column, write what you want to know about a career in computer design and about Donna. Keep those questions in mind as you read the selection. Write the answers in the L column. Then use your chart to write a summary of the selection.

Strategy Tip

Consider asking some *how* and *why* questions about the selection.

K (What I know)	W (What I want to know)	L (What I've learned)

Strategy Tip

Do you know what a computer designer does? If you do, include that information in the K column of your chart.

Donna Auguste, American Dreamer

What would your dream computer be like? You might want to take it to class. It would have to fit into your purse or backpack. You'd want it to be lightweight. You wouldn't have room for a keyboard. The computer would have to read your handwriting. Imagine such a computer. Donna Auguste not only imagined it—she also helped design it. It's called the Newton. The Apple Computer Company developed the notebook-sized computer.

Auguste's accomplishment doesn't surprise anyone who knew her as a child. She always had a great curiosity about how things worked. She dismantled doorknobs, doorbells, even toasters. In school, Auguste showed a flair for math and science. She found that some people didn't think a girl could do well in those classes. "Some of the smartest kids in my science class were girls," Auguste recalls, "but those girls did not want to let on that they understood. It was considered a boys' kind of thing."

Life changed for Auguste in the seventh grade. Her class visited a science and technology museum. For the first time, she touched a computer. Before that, she had seen computers only on television.

Computer Science:
Donna Auguste, American Dreamer

No one could explain to Auguste how computers worked. She couldn't find library books about computers, so she visited the museum often.

Auguste persuaded her mother to let her enroll in the only public high school that offered a freshman computer class. It was more than an hour away from the family home in Berkeley, California. "I was fascinated by the manner in which computers make life easier. Whatever you know how to do, computers can help you do it better."

At age 14, Auguste took on a newspaper route. She began saving for college. No one in her family had attended college, but people encouraged her to follow her dream.

Donna Auguste holds her invention, the Newton computer.

Auguste worked hard in high school. Her hard work paid off. She earned high scores on her Scholastic Aptitude Test. The University of California at Berkeley offered her a scholarship. She accepted and began her studies in computer science. Finally, she would learn just how those museum computers worked.

College life wasn't always easy. Auguste ran into **biases** against women. "When professors told students to work in teams, I had a hard time finding partners. Most of the students were males. They'd come right out and say they didn't want to work with a girl."

Auguste never considered giving up on her dreams. She earned a degree in electrical engineering and computer science. She then went to graduate school at Carnegie Mellon University.

Auguste specialized in artificial intelligence in her first job. Her team worked to develop similarities between the way humans think and the way computers work.

Auguste used that experience when she joined Apple Computers. She led a team of 20 computer experts who spent months exploring new ideas for an advanced computer. They wanted their creation to be lightweight and small. They also wanted to build a computer that could be used almost anywhere—even on a busy sidewalk!

The team members settled on what the computer should do. Then they went to work. For two and a half years, group members often worked 18 hour days, seven days a week. Their hard work paid off. The Newton was born.

Vocabulary Tip

Do you know what *biases* means? Read the other words in this paragraph for clues to its meaning.

Vocabulary Tip

The word *breakthrough* joins two words you know—*break* and *through* to make a new word. What might a *breakthrough* invention be?

Apple Computers no longer makes the Newton. However, Auguste's team's **breakthrough** invention led to a number of developments in personal-computer hardware. Some of these new computers are small enough to fit into a shirt pocket.

Today, Auguste is the head of her own company. Freshwater Technologies develops new computer and online technologies. She has four engineering patents from the U.S. Patent and Trademark Office. The Women in Technology International Hall of Fame honored her. Auguste was also featured in the PBS mini-series for children, *Science and the American Dream*. In 1998, she was named one of the 25 most influential women on the World Wide Web.

Now that you have finished reading, go back and complete the L column of your chart. Can you answer every question in the W column? What did you learn about hard work and determination from reading Auguste's story? What did you learn about computer design? The answer is your summary of the reading.

Apply It.......... To check your understanding of the reading, circle the best answer to each question below.

Test Tip

A *trait* is a characteristic. Think about the things Auguste did as a young girl. What do those actions show about her personality?

1. What trait did Donna Auguste show as a young girl?
   a. dedication
   b. cheerfulness
   c. curiosity
   d. compassion

2. Why did Auguste take on a newspaper route at age 14?
   a. She was saving for a computer.
   b. She was saving for college.
   c. She wanted to buy new clothes.
   d. Her family needed money.

3. What is the Newton?
   a. a college
   b. a museum
   c. a company that makes computers
   d. a notebook-sized computer

4. Why did some classmates refuse to work with Auguste in college?
   a. She was a woman.
   b. Members of her family had not gone to college.
   c. She did not own a computer.
   d. She had poor grades.

Computer Science:
Donna Auguste, American Dreamer

5. How did Auguste become interested in computers?
   a. Her mother showed her how to work a computer.
   b. She touched a computer in a museum.
   c. She saw a movie about computers in school.
   d. She read a book that explained how a computer works.

Use the lines below to write your answers for numbers 6 and 7. You can use your KWL chart and summary to help you.

6. Suppose you are giving Auguste the award from the Women in Technology International Hall of Fame. Write a short speech in which you honor her achievements.

   Students' speeches may mention Auguste's determination in the face of obstacles, her expertise, and her success in inventing new technologies.

7. Suppose you could design a new computer. What would it be able to do? What would it look like? How would it differ from computers currently on the market? What would you name it? Respond to the questions in paragraph form. You can also draw your computer in the space below the lines.

   Answers will vary but should include a description of the computer noting its capabilities, physical traits, and name.

Lesson 11

Real-life Math:
Balancing a Checking Account

Understand It...... In this selection, you will learn how to balance a checking account. Understanding this information will help you develop a skill that you will use often in your adult life.

You may know something about checking accounts. Maybe you have your own savings account. Try the KWL Plus strategy with this reading. It works well when you already know something about the topic.

Try It.............. Copy the KWL chart onto another piece of paper. Then list everything you know about checking accounts in the K column. Next, preview the reading, looking for numbers and unfamiliar words. In the W column, write what you want to know about checking accounts. When you finish reading, you will write what you have learned in the L column. Then you will use your KWL chart to summarize the selection.

Strategy Tip

When you think about what you know about checking accounts, think about how and why people use them.

K (What I know)	W (What I want to know)	L (What I've learned)

Balancing a Checking Account

Think about all the things adults have to pay for. Rent, insurance, groceries, telephone bills—the list goes on. Because sending cash isn't a good idea, most people use checks, which people can exchange for money.

You can open a checking account at almost any bank. You make an initial, or first, deposit. After you make your deposit, you can write checks on that money. You must record *every* check written in your record book. You note the check number; the date; the recipient, or the person who will receive it; and the amount. Then you deduct the amount of the check from the total. The remainder is the amount of money left in your account.

Your Bank Statement

Once a month, the bank will send you a statement. Your statement lists all the deposits you made during the month. It also lists all the checks that the bank has paid from your account during the month. These are your canceled checks. When you get your monthly statement, you'll want to **balance** your checkbook.

Balancing your checkbook means making sure the amount of money you have in your account is correct. If you have kept careful records of every deposit and every check, then balancing your account will be easy.

Vocabulary Tip

Notice the different forms of *balance* in the reading. One meaning of *balance* is "to make things equal."

Real-life Math:
Balancing a Checking Account

Strategy Tip

Illustrations in a math text often show how to do a process. What does this illustration show?

NUMBER	DATE	RECIPIENT OR DESCRIPTION OF DEPOSIT	(—) AMOUNT OF CHECK	✔ T	(—) CHECK FEE (IF ANY)	(+) AMOUNT OF DEPOSIT	BALANCE
	10/97	TO/FOR Deposit				49.80	49.80
							BAL 49.80
104	11/97	TO/FOR Health Life Magazine	13.50				13.50
							BAL 36.30
105	12/97	TO/FOR Sports Today	40.00				40.00
							BAL -3.70
	12/97	TO/FOR Bounced Check Fee	25.00				25.00
							BAL -28.70
	12/97	TO/FOR Deposit				100.00	100.00
							BAL 71.30

Can you follow the steps to balance this checkbook?

First, review your statement to see whether the bank deducted, or subtracted, any fees from your account. Some banks charge a service fee for operating a checking account. Then review your statement to see whether the bank added any money to your account. Many banks pay interest on the account total. Interest is a type of bonus that is added to your account for having an account at that bank.

Updating Your Total

Once you have deducted your fees and added your interest, you'll want to look over the canceled checks. Compare each check number and amount with your record book. You can make sure you wrote the correct amount of each check in your book. You can also make sure that the bank deducted the correct amount from your account.

Then mark the canceled checks. Most people put check marks next to those entries in their record book. This way, they can quickly see which checks the bank hasn't paid.

Now you are ready to see whether your account balances. Write down the account total listed in your record book. Add any deposits made to the account that are not shown on the statement. From that total, subtract the amount of total checks outstanding. The remainder should equal the amount noted in your record book. That figure is the amount of money you have in your account.

After you finish filling in the L column of your KWL chart, look over your chart. Did you answer all your W questions? Did you find information that would answer questions you didn't ask? Go ahead and make necessary changes to your chart. To make sure you understand how to balance a checkbook, use your chart to write a summary of the selection.

Apply It. . . . . To check your understanding of the selection, circle the best answer to each question below.

1. Money put into a bank account is called
   a. a check.
   b. an account.
   c. a deposit.
   d. a statement.

2. The recipient of a check is the
   a. person or company who will receive the money.
   b. date the check was written.
   c. person who has the account.
   d. amount of money in the checking account.

3. Interest is
   a. money the bank deducts from an account.
   b. money the bank adds to an account.
   c. the cost of printing your checks.
   d. a teller who pays attention to your account.

Test Tip

The word *before* shows that question 4 tests your understanding of the steps in a process. To answer this question correctly, you need to identify the first thing you do when balancing your checkbook.

4. When you balance your checkbook, what should you do before you review your canceled checks?
   a. Find the total of outstanding checks.
   b. Check the statement for service fees and interest.
   c. Note the date of the first check written from the account.
   d. Determine the total number of checks you have written.

5. What mathematical operations do you perform when you balance your checkbook?
   a. addition and division
   b. multiplication and subtraction
   c. multiplication and division
   d. addition and subtraction

Use the lines below to write your answers for numbers 6 and 7. Use your KWL chart to help you.

6. Why is it important to balance your checkbook?

   It is important to balance your checkbook so that you know exactly how much money is in your account. Students should also note that it is important that the amount taken from the account should not exceed the existing balance.

7. List the steps to follow when balancing a checkbook.

   Answers should identify the following sequence: find the updated total, find the total of outstanding checks, subtract the outstanding check total from the updated total, compare with record book total.

Real-life Math:
Lesson 12 Paying Taxes

Understand It...... You are in a store and see something you want to buy. You discover you've got just enough to buy it. However, when the clerk rings up the sale, the total is more than the cost of the item. You forgot about sales tax. In this selection, you will learn about the kinds of taxes people pay.

Use the KWL Plus reading strategy to understand this selection. Even if you don't pay taxes yet or you live in a state that doesn't have a sales tax, you've probably heard people complain about high taxes. When you work, *you* will be a taxpayer.

Try It.............. Copy the KWL chart onto another piece of paper. Then list everything you know about taxes in the K column. In the W column, write what you want to know about the topic. Think about those questions as you read. After you read, write what you've learned in the L column. Then use your KWL chart to write a summary of the selection.

Strategy Tip

Do you know what happens to the money people pay in taxes? Do you know why workers pay income taxes? You might want to include these questions in the W column of your KWL chart.

K (What I know)	W (What I want to know)	L (What I've learned)

Vocabulary Tip

The verb *levy* means "to order to pay." Notice that *charge* follows the word *levy* and tells you its meaning.

Paying Taxes

Taxes are fees that are charged by the government. The government uses tax money to cover the cost of services to the community. Schools are just one of those services. Tax money pays for maintaining roads, operating police and fire departments, running health care facilities, and defending the country.

There are many different kinds of taxes. If you have ever bought an item in a store or eaten a meal in a restaurant, you have probably paid sales tax. Most states **levy**, or charge, a fee on the sale of goods and services. The amount of tax is a certain percentage of the sale. The greater the sale's total, the more tax you pay. For example, if you buy a book that costs $14.00 in a state with 6% sales tax, you would first multiply the price of your book by the percentage that you are being taxed:

$14.00 x .06 = .84. This is your sales tax.

Then, you would add the sales tax to the price of your book.

$14.00 + .84 = $14.84

Therefore, $14.84 is the total price of your book, including the tax.

Workers pay another kind of tax, which is called income tax. In the United States, the federal government and most state governments charge workers a percentage of their salaries. A percentage of a worker's wages goes to the federal government, and another percentage goes to the state government. Some city governments also have income taxes.

Most state income taxes are proportional taxes. A proportional tax has a rate that does not change. If the rate is 6%, then every worker pays 6% of his or her income to the state, whether that income is $10,000 or $100,000. To figure out how much state tax you would pay if your income were $50,000, you would multiply your salary by the state tax.

$$\$50,000 \times .06 = \$3,000.00$$

If you earned $50,000 a year, $3,000.00 is what you would pay in tax.

Strategy Tip

This income tax form shows you how income tax is figured. Add this information to your KWL chart.

Figure your total income (See page 20.) Attach Copy B of your Forms W-2 and 10099-R here. If you didn't get a W-2, see page 25. Enclose, but do not attach, any payment with your return.	7	Wages,salaries, tips, etc. This should be shown in box 1 of your W-2 form(s). Attach Form(s) W-2				7	
	8a	**Taxable** interest income (see page 25). IF OVER $400, attach Schedule 1.				8a	
	b	**Tax-exempt** interest. DO NOT include on line 8a.		8b			
	9	Dividends. If over $400, attach Schedule 1				9	
	10a	Total IRA distributions	10a	**10b**	Taxable amount (see page 27)		
	11a	Total pensions and annuities	11a	**11b**	Taxable amount (see page 27)	11b	
	12	Unemployment compensation (see right page 30).				12	
	13a	Social security benefits.	13a	**13b**	Taxable amount (see page 31).	13b	
	14	Add lines 7 through 13b (far right column). This is your total income				**14**	
Figure your adjusted gross income	15a	Your IRA deduction (see page 34).			15a		
	b	Spouse's IRA deduction (see page 34).			15b		
	c	Add lines 15a and 15b. These are your **total adjustments.**				15c	
	16	Subtract line 15c from line 14. This is your **adjusted gross income.** If less than $25,296 and a child lived with you (less than $9,000 if a child didn't live with you), see "Earned income credit" on page 44.				16	

A part of a federal income tax form

The income tax levied by the federal government is a progressive tax. The rate of a progressive tax varies. Workers are taxed at different rates, depending on how much money they earn. A worker may pay between 15% and 39.6% of his or her taxable income to the federal government. The higher the income, the more income tax the worker pays.

For example, a worker who earns $20,000 is taxed at a rate of 15%. To figure out how much the worker would pay, multiply the salary of $20,000 by 15%, which would total $3,000.00. That is how much the worker would owe in taxes. A worker who earns $60,000 is taxed at a rate of 31%. That worker would multiply $60,000 by 31%, which would total $18,600. That is the amount of tax the worker would owe.

At the end of each year, employers send information to the IRS by April 15. At that time, people must also pay any income taxes they owe.

Now complete your KWL chart. Be sure to include all the main ideas and enough detail to write a summary of the reading.

Real-life Math:
Paying Taxes

Apply It. . . . . To check your understanding of the selection, circle the best answer to each question below.

1. A proportional tax is a tax that
   a. is paid only by wealthy members of a community.
   (b.) has a rate that does not change.
   c. has a rate that varies.
   d. is paid twice each year.

2. Which of the following statements describes how a worker's income changes the rate of federal income tax?
   a. As income increases, tax rate decreases.
   (b.) As income increases, tax rate increases.
   c. Tax rate stays the same.
   d. Tax rate varies from state to state.

3. If you buy a hammer that costs $24.00, how much extra would you have to pay if the sales tax is 5%?
   a. $.12
   (b.) $1.20
   c. $24.12
   d. $25.20

4. Which mathematical operation would you use to figure out the amount of tax a worker will pay if he earns $35,000 and the tax rate is 4%?
   a. $35.00 x .04
   b. $35,000 + .04
   (c.) $35,000 x .04
   d. $35,000 – .04

5. If a worker earns a salary of $65,000 and the state tax rate is 7%, how much state tax would the worker have to pay?
   a. $4.50
   b. $45
   c. $450
   (d.) $4,550

Use the lines below to write your answers for numbers 6 and 7. Use your KWL chart to help you.

Test Tip

To answer question 6, you must define both proportional and progressive taxes. You must also tell how they are different.

6. How is a proportional tax different from a progressive tax?

   Proportional taxes have rates that do not change. Regardless of the amount of income, everyone pays the same percentage to income tax. Progressive taxes vary. People with higher incomes pay a higher percentage of their income in tax than people making lower incomes.

7. Do you think it is fair that federal income tax is a progressive tax? Give reasons for your response.

   Sample answers: No: Progressive taxes are not fair because people who make a lot of money have to pay very high income taxes. Yes: Progressive taxes are fair because people should pay tax based on how much money they make. If people make less, they pay less; if people make more, they pay more.

Unit 3 Review: **KWL Plus**

In this unit, you have practiced using the KWL Plus reading strategy. Use this strategy when you read the selection below. Use a separate sheet of paper to draw a chart, take notes, and summarize what you learn.

Hint *Remember that all reading strategies have activities for before, during, and after reading. To review these steps, look at the inside back cover of this book.*

Faster than a Speeding Bullet

If Superman travels faster than a speeding bullet, how fast does he travel? Can he beat a rocket?

Let's say you are shooting a bullet from a .22 caliber rifle. Once you pull the trigger, the bullet travels at 1,300 feet per second. Because a mile is 5,280 feet, that bullet is moving at about a quarter mile each second.

To find miles per hour, you multiply 1,300 feet per second by the number of seconds per hour, or 3,600. So, $1,300 \times 3,600 = 4,680,000$ feet per hour. To decide how many miles per hour that is, you divide 4,680,000 by 5,280—the number of feet in a mile. The bullet is traveling at 886.4 miles an hour, so Superman has to be traveling faster than that.

The SST, or Super Sonic Transport, travels very fast. The Concorde is a commercial SST. It is an airplane that travels faster than the speed of sound. Sound travels through air at 742 miles an hour.

A regular jet passenger plane travels at about 600 miles an hour. The Concorde moves at about 1,300 miles an hour. That is quite a bit faster than sound travels in air.

Sometimes you hear speed referred to as Mach 2 or Mach 3. That measurement is named for an Austrian physicist and philosopher named Ernst Mach. He lived from 1838 to 1916 and worked with theories of flight and ballistics, which is the study of the motion and force of projectiles such as bullets.

The Mach number is calculated by determining the ratio of the speed of an object to the speed of sound in the medium through which the object is traveling. For example, the Concorde travels at Mach 1.8. That is calculated this way: Concorde's speed divided by the speed of sound through air equals the Mach number. As an equation, that would be:

$$1,300 \div 742 = \text{Mach } 1.8$$

The Concorde, for example, travels at 1.8 times the speed of sound. When an airplane or rocket exceeds the speed of sound, it creates a shock wave. Bystanders hear that shock wave as a sonic boom.

Unit 3 Review: KWL Plus

A rocket travels even faster than a Concorde. For a rocket to blast off into space, it needs to break free of Earth's gravitational pull. That speed is called the escape velocity. To take off, a rocket has to have an escape velocity of 25,000 miles an hour.

Let's say, though, that your rocket is on Venus, not Earth. Venus has less mass than Earth and has a smaller gravitational pull. To blast off from Venus and into space, your rocket would need to travel only 22,883 miles an hour. On Jupiter, which has more mass, you would need a heavy-duty rocket because the escape velocity from Jupiter is 134,548 miles an hour.

While that might sound impressive, consider this: to travel faster than light, that rocket would need to travel at 669,600,000 miles an hour!

Use your notes and charts to help you answer the questions below.

1. What is the correct ranking of these objects from slowest to fastest?
    a. bullet, Concorde, commercial jet, rocket
    b. commercial jet, bullet, Concorde, rocket
    c. Concorde, bullet, commercial jet, rocket
    d. rocket, Concorde, bullet, commercial jet

2. What is escape velocity?
    a. The speed that a rocket must reach to escape the pull of a planet's gravity.
    b. The speed at which a rocket can blast off from Earth.
    c. A number that is always fixed, regardless of where you are in the universe.
    d. both a and c

3. Ernst Mach was
    a. the person who devised the Mach number.
    b. an Australian physicist and philosopher.
    c. the person for whom the Mach number was named.
    d. both b and c

4. Why would you need a stronger rocket to travel from Jupiter than from Earth?

Jupiter is a more massive planet than Earth. Therefore, Jupiter has a larger gravitational pull and a higher escape velocity.

5. Explain how you would figure the Mach speed of an airplane.

To figure out the Mach speed of an airplane, take the speed of the airplane and divide it by the speed of sound traveling through air.

Unit 4 Strategy: **Concept Building**

Understand It......
The reading strategy called Concept Building is especially useful for math and science readings. It is based on the idea that when you read these subjects, you must know one concept, or idea, before you move on. For example, if you can't add, you'll have trouble learning multiplication. When you use Concept Building, you learn each term or concept as it is presented. Then, review what you have learned. This step ensures that you understand your reading.

Try It.............
The selection on the next page explains the process of sleep. Before you read, preview to see what it will be about. You will notice that the writing focuses on one main concept: the two kinds of sleep.

When you use the Concept Building strategy, you preview to find the main concept and write it. Then you read the selection. Next, you write a definition of the concept and the evidence or details that explain the concept. In math or science, you might write the steps of a process or operation. In the last step, you review what you have learned to make sure you understand the concept.

Follow along with a student who is using the Concept Building strategy to understand the selection about sleep.

Strategy Tip
This strategy is called Concept Building because you build your understanding of the reading with each column you fill in.

Step 1. Preview to find the main concept.

No matter what you read, preview the selection before you read. When you use the Concept Building strategy, you look for specific things. You look for words in boldface, or dark, type. These words often are followed by a definition or explanation. Also, look for other signs, like bullets (dots in a list), numbered lists, information in a box, or an illustration.

To use the Concept Building strategy, the student first drew the chart shown below. Then she thought about the subject and previewed the selection. This is what she thought as she previewed:

Sleep—let's see. I know it has to do with stages. There's the term REM Sleep in boldface type. It must be important. I'll write it in the Concept column. NREM Sleep is also in boldface type. I'll write that too.

Concept	Definition or Formula	Evidence or Steps	Review or Examples
REM sleep			
NREM sleep			

Concept Building

Now preview the selection below. Look for signals like boldface type and lists. Then read the selection. As you read, think about REM sleep and NREM sleep. You might want to highlight or underline any definitions or explanations you see. If you find a new concept in your reading, note it.

Vocabulary Tip

The boldface type shows you that the writer is introducing a new concept. Each concept is followed by an explanation written in parentheses.

Asleep in Seattle . . . and Singapore . . . and Senegal

As different as people are, we all have at least one thing in common. Across the world, people get sleepy when the sun goes down. They find a place to lie down, and they fall asleep.

Research on brain waves shows two kinds of sleep. **REM sleep** (Rapid Eye Movement) is close to wakefulness. **NREM sleep** (Non Rapid Eye Movement) is deeper sleep.

According to researchers, this is what happens when people sleep. First, people go through four stages of NREM sleep.

Stage 1   The person drifts between wakefulness and sleep. Muscles relax. Pulse and breathing become even.

Stage 2   Breathing and heart rate slow.

Stage 3   Breathing and heart rate slow even more. Body temperature and blood pressure drop.

Stage 4   This is the deepest sleep. Muscles relax completely. The sleeper moves little. Waking a person in stage 4 sleep is very difficult. People who say they can "sleep through an earthquake" are talking about stage 4.

During the night, a person goes through all four stages of sleep. When stage 4 is complete, the sleeper reverses the process. He or she returns to stage 3, then stage 2, then back to stage 1. A cycle takes about 70 to 90 minutes.

After that pattern, the sleeper enters REM sleep. This kind of sleep can last from 5 to 15 minutes. While in REM sleep, a person's eyes move quickly back and forth beneath closed eyelids. He or she may twitch or move restlessly.

Throughout the night, the sleeper will repeat the REM–NREM pattern. However, researchers have learned that REM sleep gets longer with each cycle, until REM sleep makes up 20 to 25 percent of sleep time each night.

Step 2. Explain the concept.

The student has already added the REM and NREM concepts to her Concept Building chart. Then she added information to the Definition column. She defined REM sleep. Add your own definition of NREM sleep to this chart. Here is what she thought as she began her chart:

The definitions for REM and NREM sleep are right after the words. I'll write the definitions of these terms in the Definition or Formula column.

Concept	Definition or Formula	Evidence or Steps	Review or Examples
REM sleep	Rapid Eye Movement close to wakefulness		
NREM sleep	Non Rapid Eye Movement deeper sleep		

Strategy Tip

The notes you write in the Evidence column should be in your own words. Putting information in your own words helps you remember it.

Step 3. Write the steps or the evidence for the concept.

Now read the selection. After you have read, write the evidence or details that explain each concept in the Evidence or Steps column. Evidence includes any information that helps you understand the concept. For this science selection, the student added the evidence that explained REM and NREM sleep. Add some additional evidence that you found to the chart.

The article gives some facts about REM and NREM sleep. I'll write those facts in the Evidence or Steps column.

Stage 2:
Heart rate slows.

Stage 3:
Body temperature drops.

Stage 4:
Body relaxes.

Concept	Definition or Formula	Evidence or Steps	Review or Examples
REM sleep	Rapid Eye Movement close to wakefulness	lasts 5 to 15 minutes sleeper's eyes twitch	
NREM sleep	Non Rapid Eye Movement deeper sleep	Stage 1: between wakefulness and sleep Stage 2: __(see__ Stage 3: __answers__ Stage 4: __at left)__	

Concept Building

Step 4. Review what you have learned.

Reviewing helps you make sure you understand what you've read. That's what the last column in the Concept Building chart is for. In science, the last column may be a summary. In math, you might try other problems to see if you understand how to use the concept. This is the way the student began filling out the last column in her chart.

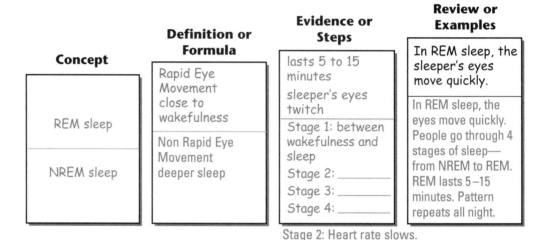

Stage 2: Heart rate slows.
Stage 3: Body temperature drops.
Stage 4: Body relaxes.

Apply It............. Try the Concept Building strategy on a reading assignment you have that presents one or two concepts. First, preview to find the concept. Then read, looking for a definition of the concept. If you are allowed to write in the book, you might highlight or underline important information. If you are not allowed to write in the book, jot down a few notes to help you locate the information later.

When you have finished reading, write any information you found that explains the concept in the Evidence or Steps column. Finally, write a review of what you have learned in the Review or Examples column. Test yourself to be sure you *do* understand. Try writing a summary. If the concept is a formula, try using the formula on another problem.

Number Sense:
Lesson 13 Understanding Remainders

Understand It...... Years ago you learned how to divide. You discovered that some numbers are not evenly divisible by other numbers. You saw that some final answers have a remainder. In this selection, you will learn more about remainders. You will recognize relationships between remainders and the final answer.

Try It.............. The Concept Building strategy will help you understand these relationships. As you preview the article, you will see that the first paragraph is important. It defines terms that will help you as you continue to read the article. Preview the subheadings and topic sentences of each paragraph.

Make a copy of the Concept Building chart on a separate sheet of paper. Write the concept (remainders) in the first box. After you read, write a brief description of the term *remainder* in the second box. In the third box, describe the occasions when you might have to make a decision about remainders. Review what you have learned by writing a summary paragraph in the last box.

Strategy Tip

You might want to change the name of the third box in the chart from *Evidence or Steps* to *Description* for this article.

Concept	Definition or Formula	Evidence or Steps	Review or Examples

Vocabulary Tip

In math, the *dividend* is the number being divided. The *divisor* is the number by which the dividend is being divided. What word do you see *inside* both of these words?

Understanding Remainders

A remainder is something that is left over. In math, the answer to a division problem can have a remainder. That occurs when a **divisor** does not go into a **dividend** evenly. Something remains, or is left over.

In your everyday life, you will solve many division problems. Often, these problems will have a remainder. In many real-life situations, the remainder must be interpreted. Sometimes, a remainder will mean that you will add 1 to the final answer. At other times, the remainder can be ignored. How will you know what to do? You will learn to look at the problem situation to see what to do about the remainder.

The Craft Fair

Millville High is having a craft fair. Kyle wants to sell birdhouses at the fair. He uses 2 meters of wire in every birdhouse he makes. The week before the fair, Kyle discovers he has 9 meters of wire. He wants to

Number Sense: Understanding Remainders

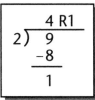

```
    4 R1
2) 9
  -8
   1
```

```
     13 R4
12) 160
    12
    40
    36
     4
```

find out how many birdhouses he can make. Kyle divides 9 by 2. His answer is 4 Remainder 1. Kyle thinks about the remainder. How many birdhouses can he make? The remainder represents part of a birdhouse. He realizes that he should ignore the remainder. Kyle discovers that he can make four birdhouses.

Sue also wants to sell crafts at the fair. She decides to make 20 photograph albums. Sue already has most of the materials she needs. She needs only 8 inches of lace for each album. Sue multiplies 20 by 8 to figure out how much lace to buy. She needs 160 inches of lace.

Sue then visits a local craft shop. The shop sells lace only by the foot. Sue divides 160 by 12. Her answer is 13 Remainder 4. Sue knows the shop will not sell less than a foot of lace. So she adds 1 to the 13. She purchases 14 feet of lace. Now she has enough lace for all 20 albums.

The two craftmakers faced similar situations. The answers to their division problems had remainders. Both crafters had to decide what to do with the remainder. They thought about the relationship between the remainder and the situation in the problem. Kyle realized that he should ignore the remainder. Sue realized that she needed to add 1 to her final answer. Different situations call for different actions.

The Competition

Three bands from Millville are going to a competition. The band directors need to order buses for the event. A total of 405 band members will attend. Each bus can hold 48 people. So one director divides 405 by 48. Her quotient is 8 Remainder 21. What should she do with the remainder? Should she ignore it? Or should she add 1 to 8?

Think about the relationship between the remainder and the problem situation. The dividend is the total number of band members attending the competition. The divisor is the number of members who can ride on each bus. So the whole number in the quotient shows how many buses are full. The remainder shows how many band members are left over. However, these people still need a ride. Therefore, the group needs nine buses to travel to the competition. Eight of the buses will be full. The ninth bus will carry only 21 members.

Suppose the director had ignored the remainder. Twenty-one band members would have been left on the sidewalk! Luckily for them, the director understood remainders.

Now that you have finished reading the selection, think about what you have read. Then review what you have learned from your Concept Building chart. You might note how you use remainders in your everyday life. You might also note the definitions of the math terms *dividend* and *divisor*.

Apply It. . . . . To check your understanding of the selection, circle the best answer to each question below.

1. The main idea of this selection is that
   a. every remainder can be ignored.
   b. whenever you have a remainder, you should add 1 to the final answer.
   c. a remainder must be interpreted.
   d. a remainder means you made a mistake.

2. What does the word *remainder* mean in this selection?
   a. an odd number
   b. a number you can divide evenly
   c. something that you can ignore
   d. something that is left over

Test Tip

Question 3 asks you about opinions. An *opinion* is a person's thoughts or feelings about a subject. The correct answer is a statement that cannot be proven true.

3. Which of the following statements is an opinion?
   a. Band competitions are enjoyable events.
   b. Sue bought 14 feet of lace.
   c. Some crafters keep a supply of materials available.
   d. The group needs nine buses to travel to the competition.

4. What would have happened if Sue had ignored her remainder?
   a. She would only have been able to make 19 albums.
   b. She would have been able to make all 20 albums.
   c. She would have made too many albums.
   d. She would have made too few albums.

5. The band director orders nine buses. That means she
   a. has not ordered enough buses.
   b. knows that having a remainder can mean adding 1 to a final answer.
   c. knows that remainders are not important in ordering buses.
   d. has ordered too many buses.

Use the lines below to write your answers for numbers 6 and 7. Use your Concept Building chart to help you.

6. Describe two real-life situations when a remainder could be ignored.

Answers will vary but may include finding the number of items a crafter needs to sell to cover the cost of supplies, identifying the lowest grade needed to maintain a certain average, or finding the fewest number of tickets that fair organizers must sell to make a profit.

7. Describe a real-life situation in which a person should add 1 to a final answer.

Answers will vary but may include determining the number of tables that must be set up to accommodate a large number of people, finding how many muffins to order so that each person has one, or finding how much soda to buy so that each member of a team has a drink.

Lesson 14

Understanding Scale: Reading a Map Scale

Understand It...... Your family has decided to travel across the country by car. An important part of planning the trip is choosing a route. You volunteer for that job. You'll probably use maps to find the best roads to take. The maps will also help you find the shortest route. In this selection, you will learn about how to read a map, a skill you will use many times in your life.

Try It.............. The Concept Building strategy will make it easier to understand this selection. Start by copying the Concept Building chart shown below on a sheet of paper. Then preview the selection. When you see the equations, you'll know they could help you define the concept. After you read, write a definition of map scale in the Definition or Formula box. Then write the steps for calculating a map scale in the Evidence or Steps box. Finally, check your understanding by practicing using a map scale in the Review or Examples box.

Strategy Tip

If the main concept is a formula for solving a problem, explain it in your own words. That will help you remember the formula.

Concept	Definition or Formula	Evidence or Steps	Review or Examples

Vocabulary Tip

What does *relative* mean in this reading? How does the meaning differ from the meaning of the word in the sentence "Aunt Jane is my favorite relative"?

Reading a Map Scale

A map is a flat drawing of an area. There are many different kinds of maps. You might have a map of your school attached to a notebook. A map of the United States might be displayed in your classroom. You may have used a map of a large amusement park to get to a favorite ride—or even to get to the amusement park.

Maps show the locations of places. Some maps show the **relative** positions of places. Those maps simply show that one item is north—or south, west, or east—of another. An amusement park map probably shows relative position. It would show that the roller coaster is south of the carousel or that the ice cream stand is east of the main gate.

Other maps are drawn to scale. That means that distances between places on the map represent the real distances between the places. How does a mapmaker show hundreds of miles on a small piece of paper? He or she uses a map scale.

A map scale is usually at the bottom of the map. The scale is a line segment marked with numbers. The numbers show the number of miles or kilometers the segment represents.

The map scale below is from a road map. It shows that 1 inch on the map represents a distance of 20 miles. The reader can use that information to determine the actual distance between two locations on the map.

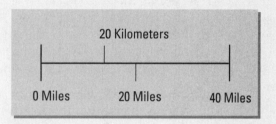

Suppose that Centerville and Maple Run are two locations on the map. The map distance between the two places is 2 inches. To find the actual distance, you write a proportion.

$$\frac{1 \text{ inch}}{20 \text{ miles}} = \frac{2 \text{ inches}}{d}$$

In this proportion, d stands for the actual distance between Centerville and Maple Run. To solve for d, multiply 20 by 2. Divide the product, 40, by 1. The result is 40. This means that the actual distance between the locations is 40 miles.

Suppose Harleytown and Elmwood are also on the map. The map distance between them is 3.5 inches. Again, you use a proportion to find the actual distance.

$$\frac{1 \text{ inch}}{20 \text{ miles}} = \frac{3.5 \text{ inches}}{d}$$

To solve for d, multiply 3.5 by 20. Divide the product, 70, by 1. The result is 70. You know that the actual distance between the locations is 70 miles.

You can use this process any time you need to find the actual distance between locations. Just make sure to check the map scale. Each map has its own scale. On a map of a small area, such as your town, 1 inch can represent 1 mile. On a map of a large area, such as your state, 1 inch can represent 50 miles. The ratio changes from map to map. However, the way you use the scale to find actual distances remains the same.

Understanding Scale:
Reading a Map Scale

Now that you know how to use a map scale, go back and complete your Concept Building chart. Be sure to add all of the steps described in the selection. Then use that information to practice calculating a map scale in the Review or Examples box.

Apply It . . . . To check your understanding of the selection, circle the best answer to each question below.

1. How are all maps alike?
   a. All maps have a map scale.
   b. All maps show distances in inches.
   c. All maps show the locations of places.
   d. All maps have a map scale and show distances in inches.

2. Which of the following is a true statement?
   a. A map that shows the relative positions of places is always drawn to scale.
   b. All maps show the actual distance between locations.
   c. All maps are drawn to scale.
   d. A map scale can be used to determine the actual distance between locations.

3. What information is given in a map scale?
   a. the number of towns shown on the map
   b. the number of people who live in the area
   c. the date the map was drawn
   d. the actual distance the scale represents

Test Tip

A *conclusion* is a statement that summarizes the key points of a reading. Which choice in question 4 sums up the main points of this selection?

4. What conclusion can you reach after reading the selection?
   a. Being able to use a map scale is a valuable life skill.
   b. Map scales are unnecessary.
   c. Only drivers need to know how to use a map scale.
   d. Every map should have the same map scale.

5. In order to find the real distance between two places on a map, you must know
   a. how many people live in the locations.
   b. the distance a segment of the scale represents.
   c. who created the map.
   d. both a and b

Use the lines on the next page to write your answers for numbers 6 and 7. Use your Concept Building chart to help you.

6. How does a map that shows relative position differ from a map that is drawn to scale?

A map that shows relative position shows the location of one place in relation to another. A map drawn to scale shows the actual distances between locations.

7. Find a map that has a scale. Choose two places shown on the map that are not too close together. Use the map scale to find the distance between these two places. Describe how you did this on the lines below.

Answers should demonstrate an ability to apply the formula given in the reading.

Lesson 15

Analyzing Data: Sample a Survey

Understand It...... Have you ever been stopped in a mall or contacted by telephone and asked to give your opinion about something? If you have, you took part in a survey. Surveys are a common way of finding out what people like and dislike. Businesses use that information to plan new products or change existing ones.

Try It............. You can conduct your own survey. Copy the Concept Building chart shown below. After you preview the selection, write the survey topic in the *Concept* box. Then write a definition of what a survey is and why it is done. Write the steps for conducting a survey in the *Evidence or Steps* box. Use your notes to write a summary in the *Review or Examples* box.

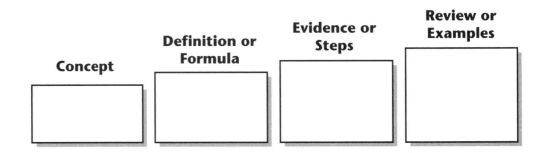

Concept | **Definition or Formula** | **Evidence or Steps** | **Review or Examples**

Sample a Survey

You have probably read or heard about the results of a survey. A survey taker asks a number of people what they think about something. Some surveys ask for opinions about a candidate running for office. Some surveys ask questions about a company's new product. Some surveys gather information about the kind of people who live in a community.

People conduct surveys for different reasons. However, all surveys have the same purpose—to collect information.

Many people think that conducting a survey is as easy as asking a bunch of questions. Wrong! A good survey is the result of a series of carefully planned steps. Asking a person a particular question is just one part of the process.

Step 1: Decide on a Topic

Every survey explores a certain topic. To identify the topic, you must think about the reason for the survey. Think about what you will do with the information you collect.

Let's say you're thinking about opening a new ice cream shop in your town. You need to decide how much to charge for each item sold.

You need to charge enough to make a profit. You also want the prices to be fair to your customers. A survey could help you set prices. You could conduct a survey to find how much a person in your community is willing to spend for an ice cream cone.

Step 2: Identify the Sample

The people who respond to a survey make up the sample. A sample is a small group that represents the opinions of a much larger group.

It's **unlikely** that you could ask everyone in your town how much an ice cream cone should cost. However, you could survey a small number of those people. You could survey all the high school students or everyone who drives a car.

Would those groups represent all the members of your community? No. People other than students and drivers buy ice cream. Their opinions would not be included in the survey.

A better sample would be every fifth person who leaves the library or every person who attended a school carnival. Those samples would be a broader selection of community members.

Step 3: Decide on the Survey Method

People gather information in three ways. In a mail survey, sample members receive a list of questions in the mail. In a telephone survey, sample members answer questions over the phone. In a personal survey, an interviewer asks the sample members questions in person.

Step 4: Write the Questions

The most important part of conducting a survey is writing the questions. The questions must be clear. They must be easy to understand. They must focus on the topic being explored. Most important, they should not influence the response.

Suppose you ask this question in your ice cream price survey: "Should an ice cream cone cost $1.00 or $1.50?" Does it put a limit on the answer? Yes! A person can respond in only two ways: either $1.00 or $1.50. Maybe the person feels that $1.25 is a fair price. As written, the question does not allow that answer. The person answering the question can't give an honest opinion. A better survey question would be "What do you think is a fair price for an ice cream cone?"

Step 5: Ask the Questions

Now it is time to ask the questions. You've chosen the method of asking questions and contacted the members of the sample. You give them time to respond. Then you collect the responses.

Vocabulary Tip

The prefix *un-* means "not," so *unlikely* means "not likely." Knowing the meaning of a prefix can help you define an *un*known word.

Analyzing Data:
Sample a Survey

Step 6: Analyze the Data

You count the responses to each survey question. Frequent responses are identified. Sometimes, graphing or charting the results makes them clearer. You think about what you learn from your survey.

The results of the ice cream survey might show that 28 of 50 people said that $1.25 is a fair price for an ice cream cone. Another 17 people said that $1.50 is a fair price. Since those were the top two responses, you might decide to charge $1.35 for a cone.

After you finish reading about surveys, complete your Concept Building chart. Then use your notes to write a summary of the selection. The summary should include the important points and details to back them up. Then look over your notes and summary one last time.

Your next step is to conduct a survey of your own. Pick a topic that interests you. Then follow the steps to gather your information. Share your findings with your class.

Apply It.. . . . . To check your understanding of the selection, circle the best answer to each question below.

1. What is the purpose of every survey?
    a. to gather information
    b. to analyze information
    c. to identify a topic
    d. to create questions

2. A sample is
    a. the topic of the survey.
    b. a method of questioning.
    c. a small group of people who represent a larger group.
    d. a way of analyzing information.

3. Which of the following is *not* true of a good survey question?
    a. easy to understand
    b. focused on the topic being explored
    c. clearly written
    d. influences the response

Test Tip

The selection describes the steps in a process. Question 4 asks about the order of those steps. You probably have the steps in order in your Concept Building chart.

4. According to the selection, what should you do immediately before writing the survey questions?
    a. Identify the sample.
    b. Decide on the survey method.
    c. Find a survey topic.
    d. Contact members of the sample group.

5. How might a chart or graph help you analyze survey results?
   a. Looking at a picture is more enjoyable than looking at words.
   b. Data on a chart or a graph is easy to see and comprehend.
   c. Charts and graphs are colorful.
   d. Looking at words can be boring.

Use the lines below to write your answers for numbers 6 and 7. Use your Concept Building chart to help you.

6. Name three surveys that you or someone you know has participated in or heard about. How were they alike? How did they differ?

Answers will vary but should note that the topics of the surveys differed. Therefore, the types of questions differed. The purpose of each of the surveys was to collect information.

7. Graph or chart the results of the survey you conducted. If you want to show similarities or differences, try a bar graph. If you want to show how something changed over time, choose a line graph. You can use the space below the lines to draw your graph or chart. Then describe how you made your graph or chart.

Charts and graphs will vary but should demonstrate an understanding of ways to visually express data.

Word Problems:
Lesson 16 Finding Unit Rate

Understand It...... Most people try to get the best value for their dollars. This selection explores a math skill that is used by smart shoppers. It will help you get the most for your money. Concept Building is a good strategy to use with this selection because it is about one concept: figuring out unit rate.

Try It.............. On a separate sheet of paper, draw a Concept Building chart like the one shown below. Write the concept in the Concept box. Then preview the selection. Look for information that helps you understand the concept. You might highlight or underline the information so you can find it easily.

After you read, write a definition of the concept in the Definition or Formula box. Add details that explain the concept or the steps for finding the unit rate to the Evidence or Steps box. Finally, review what you have learned in the Review or Examples box.

Strategy Tip

Think about what you know about comparing prices. This information will help you prepare to understand what you read.

Concept	Definition or Formula	Evidence or Steps	Review or Examples

Vocabulary Tip

The suffix -er means "one who does a certain action." A consumer is "one who consumes" and a shopper is "one who shops." Suffixes can help you understand new words.

Finding Unit Rate

Every person who has ever bought an item in a store is a **consumer**. Most people try not to waste their hard-earned money.

A wise consumer is a comparison **shopper**. A comparison shopper compares the prices of products to figure out which item is the best buy. To compare prices, a shopper needs to find the unit rate of each product. Unit rate is the cost for one unit of an item. For example, a 20-ounce box of cereal costs $3.40. The unit rate for that product is the cost for one ounce, or one unit, of cereal.

Many grocery stores display labels on the shelves that show the unit rate of their products. That helps consumers compare prices. Other kinds of stores don't usually supply that information. Sometimes, consumers must find the unit rate on their own. Applying this math skill to everyday life situations can help consumers use their money wisely.

The first step in finding unit rate is to set up a ratio. The ratio identifies the two variables being compared. In the cereal example, the variables are the cost of a box of cereal and the number of ounces per box. The ratio is:

$$\frac{\text{cost}}{\text{ounces}} = \frac{3.40}{20}$$

Strategy Tip

When you preview math selections, look carefully at the problems that are worked out. They will help you understand the concept.

Once the ratio is set up, divide to find the cost of a single unit. In this example, the single unit is one ounce of cereal. So, $3.40 is divided by 20. The quotient is $0.17. Therefore, the unit rate is $0.17. That is the cost of one ounce of cereal.

Suppose a 32-ounce box of the same cereal costs $4.80. Finding the unit rate of the product shows which size is the best buy. Again, set up a ratio that identifies the variables being compared. For the 32-ounce size, the ratio is:

$$\frac{\text{cost}}{\text{ounces}} = \frac{\$4.80}{32}$$

The next step is to divide to find the cost of one unit. Since $4.80 divided by 32 is $0.15, the unit rate is $0.15 per ounce. Comparing the two unit rates shows you that the larger box is a better buy.

Unit rate can provide valuable information in other real-life situations, too. Finding unit rate can show gas mileage, or the distance a car travels on one gallon of gasoline. The driver must first know how much gas the gas tank holds. Then he or she must find the total distance the car can travel on that gas.

Strategy Tip

Here, the author gives you another example of unit rate. Work the problem out as you read to be sure you know how to find the unit rate.

Suppose a driver fills the car's tank with gasoline. The driver knows that the car has a 16-gallon tank. He or she notes the odometer reading when the tank is filled. The odometer shows how far the car has traveled. When the tank is empty, the driver checks the odometer reading again. It shows that the car has traveled 368 miles.

The driver then sets up a ratio. The variables are the number of miles driven (368) and the number of gallons of gasoline (16). Then the driver divides 368 by 16 to find the quotient 23. The unit rate shows that the car has gotten 23 miles per gallon of gasoline.

There are many other possible ways to use unit rate. It can determine how fast a runner runs. It can show the production rate of a machine. Unit rate can even be used to make predictions about how much food and drink a large group of people would need. Figuring out unit rate is a math skill that a person can use again and again.

Now create your Concept Building chart. In the Review or Examples box, construct a unit rate problem and solve it.

Word Problems: Finding Unit Rate

Apply It. . . . . To check your understanding of the reading, circle the best answer to each question below.

1. According to the selection, a wise consumer
   a. shops at many different stores.
   (b.) compares prices of products.
   c. knows how to divide.
   d. enjoys performing mathematical calculations.

Test Tip

Every sentence in a selection is related to the main idea. To correctly answer question 2, find the statement that connects to all the sentences in the selection.

2. What is the main idea of the selection?
   (a.) Finding unit rate is a skill that has many real-life applications.
   b. Every car owner should know how to find unit rate.
   c. Division is an important math skill.
   d. Finding unit rate is a complicated process.

3. What does the unit rate tell a shopper?
   a. the total cost of an item
   b. the total weight of an item
   (c.) the cost for one unit of an item
   d. the weight of one unit of a product

4. What is the tone of the selection?
   a. humorous
   b. mysterious
   c. persuasive
   (d.) informative

5. What is gas mileage?
   (a.) the distance a car travels on one gallon of gasoline
   b. the amount of gasoline used during a long trip
   c. the number of miles a car has traveled
   d. the amount of gasoline a car's gas tank can hold

Use the lines below to write your answers for numbers 6 and 7. Use your Concept Building chart to help you.

6. List two real-life situations in which finding unit rate would help you.

Sample answer: Unit rate can be applied when figuring the amount of food needed for a party or the cost per ounce of a box of cereal.

7. A 24-ounce box of cereal costs $3.60. Explain how you would find the unit rate for one ounce of cereal.

Students should describe how they set up a ratio of $3.60 (cost) divided by 24 ounces to find a unit rate of 15 cents.

Unit 4 Review: Concept Building

In this unit, you have practiced using the Concept Building reading strategy. Use this strategy when you read the selection below. Use a separate sheet of paper to draw a chart, take notes, and summarize what you learn.

Hint *Remember that all reading strategies have activities for before, during, and after reading. To review these steps, look at the inside back cover of this book.*

The Line on Geometry

From the time of the ancient Egyptians and Babylonians, people have used geometry. In ancient times, geometry was mainly concerned with very basic information. People wanted to find ways to create straight angles so that buildings would be straight.

The 6th-century Greek mathematician Pythagoras was the father of scientific geometry. Pythagoras was born on the island of Samos, but he left because of his dislike for the tyrannical leader Polycrates. About 550 B.C., he settled in southern Italy. The movement he founded there was based on his religious, political, and philosophical beliefs. Today, everything that we know about Pythagoras comes from his followers.

Pythagoras and his group made major contributions to the study of mathematics and geometry. One of his most famous contributions is the equation $a^2+b^2=c^2$. This equation is called the Pythagoreon Theorem, which states that the square of the hypotenuse of a right triangle is equal to the sum of the squares of the other two sides.

Other Greeks contributed to the study of geometry too. Perhaps the most famous geometry textbook ever written is Euclid's *Elements*. Despite his lack of sophisticated knowledge or techniques, Euclid was able to create a textbook for geometry that served as the basis for the study of geometry up to the present day.

From the time of the ancient Greeks to the end of the Middle Ages, there was little groundbreaking work done in geometry. Then, in the 16th century, the French thinker René Descartes published his important work *A Discourse on Method.* Descartes was able to show the relationship between geometry and algebra. He showed how the methods used in algebra could be used by geometry, and vice versa. This work is the basis of analytic geometry, which in turn is the basis for much of the work in geometry today.

Unit 4 Review: Concept Building

In analytic geometry, the figures of geometry—lines, curves, shapes—can be represented by a table of halves, or an algebraic equation, and a graph in a coordinate system. A student can locate a point in three-dimensional space with a set of coordinates.

Descartes's breakthrough of using numbers to describe geometric positions was also responsible in part for advanced work in calculus and other fields in higher mathematics.

Another branch of geometry, descriptive geometry, is the basis for much work in engineering and architecture today. To do their jobs, architects and engineers often must rely on making accurate two- and three-dimensional models that demonstrate the relationship of these forms in space.

Use your notes and charts to help you answer the questions below.

1. Euclid's *Elements* is notable because
   a. it was the first geometry textbook used by the Greeks.
   (b.) it was used as a textbook for geometry.
   c. it went against the established wisdom of the time.
   d. it was the basis for the Pythagorean Theorem.

2. René Descartes was important to the field of geometry because
   (a.) he linked geometry and algebra.
   b. his textbook is still used today.
   c. he invented descriptive geometry.
   d. both b and c

3. Architects and engineers use descriptive geometry because
   a. it allows them to represent three-dimensional models accurately.
   b. it is useful when designing buildings.
   c. it is the basis of geometry.
   (d.) both a and b

4. Explain the importance of Pythagoras to the field of geometry.

   Pythagoras was the father of scientific geometry. He developed the Pythagorean Theorem: $a^2 + b^2 = c^2$.

   _____

5. Describe some of the uses of geometry today.

   Sample answer: Architects must have a strong understanding of geometry when designing buildings.
   Geometry is also used when playing miniature golf. Knowledge of geometric angles can help a golfer
   figure out exactly where to direct the ball.

Vocabulary Strategies

How do you define a word you do not know? You may already use a method. For example, you may look for how a word is used in a sentence. In this handbook, you will learn some new methods of understanding word meanings. You may also review methods you already know.

Using Graphics to Understand Unknown Words

One method of finding the meaning of an unknown word is to use a word map. This method makes sense when the word is important in the selection. When you skim a selection and realize you need to understand a word, it may be worthwhile to create a word map based on this word.

For example, you may be reading a math selection about computers. To understand what you are reading, you need to understand what the words *Central Processing Unit* mean. First, preview the selection. As you preview, look for information about the words. Look for photos, captions, charts, or other illustrations. As you read, look for the ways the words are used in the selection. Here is an example of a word map about a computer's Central Processing Unit:

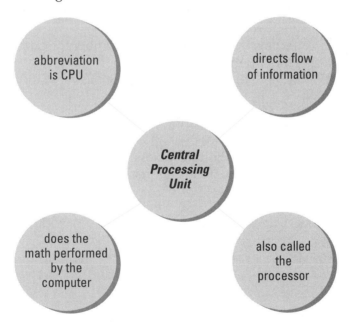

The reader who made this word map knows that the Central Processing Unit of a computer directs the flow of information into and through the computer, that it does the math performed by the computer, and that it may also be referred to as the CPU or processor. Now he or she can read with greater understanding.

In these exercises, you will learn about ways to figure out the meanings of the words you read.

Exercise 1   Direction Words

Understand It...... There are some words you need to know to succeed in school. Below is a list of common words you will see in textbooks and test questions and what each one means.

Describe—create a clear picture	**Discuss**—present ideas about a topic
Explain—give facts or reasons	
List—give examples	**Analyze**—explain in depth how things are related to one another
Compare—show similarities	
Contrast—show differences	**Identify**—place a person or event in time
Illustrate—give examples	
Summarize—state important points	**Define**—give the meaning of

Try It.............. To check your understanding of the direction words, circle the best answer to each question below.

1. When you compare two plays, what should you do?
    a. Write how they are the same.
    b. Write how they are the same and how they are different.
    c. Describe both plays.
    d. Write how the plays are different.

2. The word *summarize* means
    a. to create a vivid picture of the story.
    b. to show differences.
    c. to state the important points.
    d. to explain how things are related.

First, underline the direction word. Then provide an answer.

3. Describe your classroom. _____

    The direction word is *describe*. Students should create a clear picture of the classroom.

    _____

4. List five holidays. _____

    The direction word is *list*. Students' list of holidays might include President's Day, Independence Day, or Thanksgiving.

5. Explain how to get from your classroom to the cafeteria. _____

    The direction word is *explain*. Students should give directions from their classroom to the cafeteria.

    _____

Exercise 2   Context Clues: Part I

Understand It...... One of the ways good readers figure out the meaning of words they do not know is by using context clues.

- **Look at the words around the one you do not know.** Looking at the words around the one you do not understand will give you clues to the word's meaning. Read the following selection:

> Mr. McHenry is the school's biggest **benefactor**. Every year, he gives a large sum of money to our school, and this year was no different. Mr. McHenry gave his biggest donation yet.

The words and sentences around *benefactor* give you clues as to its meaning. Mr. McHenry gave money to the school. The school received another donation this year. Mr. McHenry is referred to as a *benefactor*. So you can conclude that a *benefactor* is someone who donates money.

- **Look for all the times the word is used.** Sometimes a word you don't know is repeated. Look at all the places the word is used for more clues.

Read this paragraph. Use clues to understand the words in bold type.

> When plants and animals die, they **decompose**. Bacteria and fungi eat them. As the plants and animals **decompose**, or break down into smaller parts, the decay frees nutrients that make the soil rich. The nutrients will help the plants grow, completing the food chain.

Try It.............. To check your understanding of the word *decompose*, circle the best answer to each question below.

1. When plants and animals decompose, they
   a. eat bacteria and fungi.
   b. break down into parts.
   c. ruin the soil.
   d. both a and b

2. *Decompose* means
   a. to grow plants.
   b. to decay.
   c. to complete the food chain.
   d. both a and b

3. Which of these statements is correct?
   a. Nutrients decompose into bacteria and fungi.
   b. Nutrients decompose into plants and animals.
   c. Nutrients complicate the food chain.
   d. Nutrients make the soil rich.

Exercise 3   Context Clues: Part II

Understand It...... Sometimes writers make it easy for readers to understand difficult words. They add definitions, restatements, or synonyms. They also use examples that show the word's meaning, or compare or contrast the word to other known words. Here are some of those tools:

- **Definitions, restatements, and synonyms.** If authors think a word may be difficult, often they will help their readers by defining the word. They may also restate the meaning of the word and show the meaning through a synonym. Here is an example of each:

   Definition: She studied **astronomy**, which is the study of the stars, the planets, and the universe.

   Restatement: The scientist made a **hypothesis**, or an educated guess, before beginning his experiment.

   Synonym: Dan was feeling so **elated**, so delighted, by the grade he got, that he agreed to come to the party.

- **Meaning through example.** Sometimes, authors use an example to show the meaning of a word in action. Examples may be shown by words such as *for instance, for example,* and *such as.* Here is an example:

   The scientist found different **amulets**, such as a rabbit's foot and bags of herbs, near the ancient altar.

- **Comparisons and contrasts.** A sentence may include a comparison that shows how the unknown word is like another word. The words *like, as,* and *similar to* may signal this. A contrast shows how a word is unlike another word. Look for words such as *but, however, on the contrary,* and *on the other hand* in contrasts. For example:

   Comparison: Marge was **prompt**, and because everyone else was on time, too, the meeting started at 8 A.M.

   Contrast: You may be a **hypocrite**, but the rest of the people showed that they believed what they said they believed.

Try It.............. Read the following selections. Use context clues to help you understand the meaning of the words in bold type. Then answer the questions that follow each one.

Production at the Dalls division of the Lakeland Corporation is completely **automated**. However, production at the Columbus division is done by hand.

1. Which words help you figure out the meaning of the word *automated*?
   The words *by hand* give clues to *automated.*

2. If "by hand" is the opposite of *automated*, what does *automated* mean?
   Automated means "not by hand."

> **Hieroglyphics,** which is a system of picture writing, was invented by the Egyptians. Egyptians began using **hieroglyphics,** or picture signs, to express their ideas in written form more than seven thousand years ago. The Egyptians wrote their stories and messages on a special paper that they learned to make from river reed called **papyrus.**

3. What is *hieroglyphics*?
   Hieroglyphics is a system of picture writing.

4. Which words help you figure out the meaning of *hieroglyphics*?
   Picture writing and *picture signs* give clues to the meaning of *hieroglyphics.*

5. What is *papyrus*?
   Papyrus is a paper made from a river reed.

6. What clue helped you figure out the meaning of *papyrus*?
   Paper gives a clue to the meaning of *papyrus.*

Exercise 4 Using Related Words to Find Meaning

Understand It...... Some words are easy to define if you look at their parts. Familiar words that are related in meaning can help you figure out the meaning of an unfamiliar word. For example, look at the word in bold type in this sentence.

> When you complete that **questionnaire**, don't forget to use a pencil to fill in your answers.

You may not know the word *questionnaire*. But even though the word seems long, you can decode it. One way is to look closely at the word.

You probably recognize a word within the longer word *questionnaire*. You know the word *question*. Knowing that word and looking at the sentence, you can figure out that *questionnaire* means "a paper that has some questions to answer."

Questionable is another word related to the word *question*. Knowing the word *question* and the suffix *-able* can help you figure out that *questionable* means "open to question or doubt."

Many words can be formed from the same base word, or root. These words often have related meanings. Here is how to use your knowledge of related words.

When you see a long word that you don't know, stop. Look at the word carefully. Is there a word you recognize within the longer word? Look at the word in bold type in the sentence. See if you can find a root word to decode the longer word.

> **Genetics** is one of the most interesting subjects you can learn about.

That word may seem difficult at first, but it is based on a root word you may know: *gene*. You know that the word has something to do with the kinds of things a person is born with. Knowing this is enough to be able to gain some understanding of the word's meaning. *Genetics* is the study of the kinds of characteristics people are born with.

Recognizing the root word *gene* can also help you figure out that the meaning of *geneticist* is someone who studies *genetics*.

Try It. . . . .   Read the following paragraphs. Look at the words in bold type. Use the root words you know to help you decide what the longer words mean.

> Gail waited in her dressing room, alone. This was her big night, and she needed **quietude** to get ready to go on. She had been practicing this scene for weeks. She had even been trained by a man who knew everything about how to fight with swords. Still, she did not feel ready. The swordplay in the scene made her **unbelievably** nervous. What if she hurt someone with that sharp point? What if someone hurt her?
>
> It was **finally** time to go on. Gail took a deep breath. She looked in the mirror one more time. She was ready. She threw back her head, put her sword in its sheath, and headed for the stage.

First, identify the root word. Then, circle the best answer to each question below.

1. The root word in *quietude* is: <u>quiet</u>

2. *Quietude* means
    a. getting ready.
    b. sleep.
    c. time.
    (d.) calmness.

3. The root word in *unbelievably* is: <u>believe</u>

4. The best definition for *unbelievably* is
    a. believable.
    b. barely.
    (c.) not to be believed.
    d. both b and c

5. The root word in *finally* is: <u>final</u>

6. In this example, *finally* means
    a. never.
    b. always.
    c. a nervous time.
    (d.) at last.

Exercise 5   Signal Words

Understand It . . . . . . You often see words in directions. They tell you in what order to do things and allow you to follow a reading selection more easily. Here are some of those words:

- **Words that give you steps.** You may often see these words when you are reading a science experiment. You will see them in writing that describes a process. You also will see them when you are following directions. If you put together a bike, for example, you may see a series of steps that you should take.

Some of these words are number words, such as *first*, *second*, and *last*. Others help you keep track of the order in which you should do something, such as *before* and *then*. Here is an example of how you might see these words:

> **First**, put the sugar and the water in the pan. **Second**, turn up the heat to high. **Next**, cook until the mixture bubbles. **Finally**, let it cool.

- **Words that tell you what is coming next.** Often writers will tell you what is coming next by using these signal words. You may remember seeing words such as *therefore* or *in conclusion*. These words will give you clues to what the writer is doing. Notice the signal words in the sentences below.

> Let me **restate** this point. No one is sure what this drug will do. **Therefore**, I will not approve it. **In conclusion**, I must say that no one should ever take this unsafe drug.

When you see the words *in conclusion*, you know the writer is signaling that he or she is reviewing, or summing up, the selection.

Read the paragraphs below. Use signal words to help you understand how the words in bold type are used. Then answer the questions that follow.

> If you plan to do this experiment, follow these steps. **First**, gather all of your materials. **Second**, clean your equipment well. **Last**, make sure all of your equipment is working. If you do all these things in this order, you will have done all you can to make sure your experiment will work.
>
> **In conclusion**, let me end my paper by summarizing for you the most important conclusions of my research. **First**, there is not enough information available to say if the horned bat will ever return. Even

though we have an idea that the bat has found other places to live, we do not know that for certain. **Second**, there are no plans to create a new habitat near here. **Finally**, and **most important**, there is no money to continue studying this topic. I am afraid the horned bats have to survive on their own.

Try It . . . . To check your understanding of the signal words, circle the best answer to each question below.

1. Which of these steps comes last?
   a. preparing for the experiment
   b. making sure the equipment is working
   c. cleaning the equipment well
   d. getting together all materials

2. What is the author signaling when she writes *in conclusion*?
   a. that she is briefly reviewing her findings
   b. that she is at the beginning of her arguments
   c. that this is the research that took the most time
   d. that these are the steps that listeners should follow

3. What is the *most important* conclusion of the scientist writing the second paragraph?
   a. Horned bats are extinct.
   b. There is no money left for research on the bats.
   c. No one can say if the horned bats will return.
   d. There are no new habitats for the horned bats.

4. Read the following list. Number the entries in time order.
   __2__ Second, listen for a dial tone.
   __4__ Finally, tell the dispatcher where the fire is.
   __1__ First, pick up the phone.
   __3__ After that, dial 911.

5. Number the following sentences in correct order.
   __2__ First, I missed the bus that I take to school.
   __1__ My first day of school was very hectic.
   __5__ Luckily, I found a seat in the back of class, so no one saw me come in late.
   __4__ As a result, I was 15 minutes late.
   __3__ Then, I had to wait ten extra minutes so my mom could drive me.

Exercise 6   Prefixes and Suffixes

Understand It...... A prefix is a word part that is added to the beginning of a root word. A suffix is a word part that is added to the end of a root word. These add-ons change the meaning of a word. You may already know more of these than you think. Read this sentence:

> "Did your shoes come **untied**?"

You know that word *untied* means "not tied." The prefix *un-* means "not."

The more you read, the more experienced you will become with prefixes and suffixes. Some, like *un-*, you already know. Other often-used prefixes and suffixes are worth memorizing. Here are some of the most common ones:

Prefixes	Meanings	Examples
non-, in-, im-, il-, ir	not	*Nonfiction* means "not fiction." *Illegal* means "not legal." *Impartial* means "not partial."
de-, dis-	away from or the opposite of	*Disapprove* means "the opposite of approve."
re-	again	*Regain* means "to gain again."
pre-, fore-	before or ahead of time	*Preview* means "to see before."
trans-	across or to the other side of	*Transoceanic* means "across the ocean."

Suffixes	Meanings	Examples
-less	without	*Clueless* means "without a clue."
-ful, -ous	full of	*Thankful* means "full of thanks."
-er, -or, -ist	a person or thing that does something	A *tourist* is "a person who tours."
-able, -ible	can or able to be	*Adaptable* means "able to adapt."
-ship, -ment, -ness, -hood	the state of or the condition of or the act or process of	*Parenthood* means "the state of being a parent."

Read the paragraphs below. Decide on the meaning of the words in bold type by looking at the prefixes and suffixes attached to them. Then answer the questions below.

> The **pianist** knew he was late. He was afraid that he would have to wait until the very end to perform his piece. It was a difficult arrangement. He would have to sit there and think about all the mistakes he could make. The music called for a **variable** tone. He could get that wrong. He could do so many things wrong.
>
> The concert master called his name. Slowly, the pianist rose. He was ready to tell them to **reschedule** the audition. Then one of the judges saw him and beamed. It was his old friend and teacher, Mr. Majors.

Try It............. To check your understanding of the vocabulary entries, circle the best answer to each question below.

1. The root word in *pianist* is: <u>piano</u>

2. *Pianist* means
   (a.) someone who plays the piano.
   b. the act of playing a piano.
   c. someone who does not play the piano.
   d. someone who can fix the piano.

3. The root word in *variable* is: <u>vary</u>

4. Which is the best definition of a *variable* tone?
   a. a tone that stays the same.
   b. a tone that is rich and full.
   c. a tone that is set.
   (d.) a tone that can change.

5. The root word in *rescheduled* is: <u>schedule</u>

6. If the audition had to be *rescheduled*, it would be
   a. not scheduled.
   (b.) scheduled again.
   c. able to be scheduled.
   d. in the act of being scheduled.

Apply What You Have Learned

Use the strategies you have learned in this book to analyze the following selections. If you need to review the steps of any strategy, look at the inside back cover of this book.

Use the Vocabulary Tips to help you with words that may be unfamiliar. Circle any other words that you need to define.

Math History:
Review 1

Florence Nightingale, Crusading Nurse

Have you ever visited a hospital? If so, you probably remember a very clean building. Hospital staffs work hard to keep germs from spreading. They know that cleanliness is the key to stopping the spread of infection.

That was not always the case. The hospitals of long ago were quite different. Patients' rooms had little fresh air. Supplies were few. Dirt was everywhere. It may seem odd, but scientists have only known for about 100 years that dirt and germs carry disease.

That all changed because of the hard work of a woman named Florence Nightingale. She dedicated her life to reforming medical care.

Early Life

Florence Nightingale was born on May 12, 1820, in Florence, Italy. Her parents named her after the city where she was born. Her father was a wealthy Englishman. Her mother was a strong-willed woman. She wanted Florence and her sister to live a life of social **prominence**. She wanted them to be friendly with well-known people and to go to fashionable parties. Social events were the focus of their lives.

The family moved to England when Florence was a young girl. Her mother taught her and her sister about society and running a home. Mr. Nightingale taught his daughters history and philosophy. At that time, girls rarely studied these subjects.

As a teenager, Florence was surrounded by friends and relatives. The family traveled often. However, Florence wanted a fuller life. She was not content with marrying well and raising a family. She wanted to serve others, but she wasn't sure how to start.

At the age of 22, Nightingale discovered her lifework. She learned of the Institute of Protestant Deaconesses in Kaiserswerth, Germany, which trained nurses in hospital work. Nightingale began studying health. She read all she could about caring for the sick. For two years, she hid her interest from her family. Finally, she found the courage to tell her parents. Nightingale told them she wanted to attend the institute to become a nurse.

Vocabulary Tip

Do you know what *prominence* means? Look at the sentences that follow it for clues.

A Life of Nursing

Six years later, Florence Nightingale finally got her wish. Against the will of her parents, she entered the Institute. After completing her studies, she returned to London and became director of a women's hospital. Nightingale set about changing the hospital. She made sure the patients received nutritious food. She made sure the patients' rooms had fresh air. Most important, she taught the staff how to keep the hospital clean.

Soon after Nightingale arrived at the hospital, England and France declared war on Russia. English soldiers were hurt or killed in large numbers. Nightingale wanted to do something for her countrymen. She left for the battlefield with a handful of nurses.

Nightingale was shocked at what she found. Wounded soldiers filled a filthy hospital that was short on food, supplies, and staff. Nightingale went to work. With the help of others, she scrubbed the place. She trained nurses. She made sure the patients received healthful meals. Her efforts paid off.

Within a year, the death rate fell more than 20 percent. The grateful patients nicknamed Nightingale "The lady with the lamp." She brought light and air and hope to a hospital that had been just another place to die.

Contribution to Mathematics

News of Nightingale's achievements spread. When she returned to England, she met with Queen Victoria. The British War Department asked for her advice on how to help the wounded. Nightingale wrote an 800-page report detailing her work. While preparing this report, Nightingale created the "polar-area diagram." It presented a picture of her data. Today, we know the "polar-area diagram" as a **pie chart**. It is a popular method of picturing information. Pie charts show how all of the pieces of information on a subject relate to one another.

After she sent in her report, Nightingale's health began to decline. She spent much of her time in bed. However, she still wrote about caring for the sick. She also continued to suggest hospital reforms. In 1910, Nightingale died.

Vocabulary Tip

In the term *pie chart*, think of what a pie looks like. What is its shape and how is it cut? Drawing a mental picture can help you understand a term.

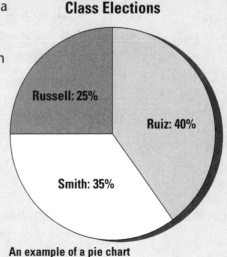

Senior Class Elections

Russell: 25%
Ruiz: 40%
Smith: 35%

An example of a pie chart

Budgeting: Managing Your Money

Vocabulary Tip

Identify is used several times in this section. What context clues can you find to help you define the word?

How often do you think about your goals? A goal is something that you want to do or accomplish. Goals are personal. Although they vary from person to person, everyone has some personal goals.

It's helpful to **identify** a goal for each area of your life. Because you are attending school, you should identify an educational goal. Many students your age already know they want to go to college. Do you? Maybe you think a trade school sounds right for you.

Financial goals are important. Financial goals identify what you hope to accomplish with your money. If you plan to go to college, saving money for your tuition might be a financial goal. Other financial goals might include saving enough money to buy a car.

After you identify a goal, you need to make a plan to achieve it. This plan will describe what you must do each day or week to reach your goal.

If your educational goal is to attend college, your plan could identify the kinds of courses you will take in high school. The plan could also include a weekly study schedule. It could even include a list of activities you should do to apply for a scholarship.

A plan for reaching your financial goal is called a budget. A budget lists exactly what you will do with the money you earn. You make a plan that shows how much money you will spend and what you will spend it on. You also make a plan that shows how much money you will save.

Making a personal budget does not require a great deal of time. Here are four easy steps to follow.

Step 1: Identify Your Income

Your income is all the money that you receive regularly. For most teens, income has two sources: earnings and allowance. List your sources of money and how much you receive. Don't include gift money. That's not a regular source of income.

Add the figures together to find your total income. You can figure out your weekly income, monthly income, or yearly income.

Step 2: Identify Your Expenses

The money you spend is your expenses. Expenses may include food, clothing, school supplies, personal care items, and entertainment. List all of the ways you usually spend money. Note the average amount you spend on each item. Add the figures to find your total expenses.

Step 3: Savings

Your savings is the money you put aside for future use. Most people put their savings into bank accounts. A bank account earns **interest**. Interest is money the bank gives to its account holders. The amount of interest is a percentage of the total amount of money you have in your account. Money placed in a savings account earns money.

Step 4: Balance Your Budget

Now you know how much money you receive, how much you spend, and how much you want to save. Your next step is to make sure your budget is balanced. Add your expenses and your savings. If your income equals the sum of your expenses and your savings, your budget is balanced.

If your income is less than your expenses, you need to rework your budget. You do not receive enough money to cover your expenses and savings. If your income is greater than your expenses, you can increase either your expenses or your savings.

After you create a balanced budget, you must follow your plan. For some people, that is difficult. However, if you do stick to your budget, you'll reach your personal financial goals.

Vocabulary Tip

In banking, *interest* is "money paid or received on an account." What other meanings do you know for the word *interest*?

Vocabulary Tip

The *horizontal* axis runs straight across the bottom of a graph, like the horizon. The *vertical* axis runs straight up and down.

Most people understand visual information easily. That's one reason why businesses, schools, and governments use graphs. A graph is a visual display of information. Signs and symbols represent ideas.

There are many kinds of graphs. A bar graph lets a viewer compare data. Bars of different heights show different data.

The bar graph on this page shows the number of students involved in some clubs at Maple Shade High School. The **horizontal** axis, which runs across the bottom of the graph, says "Clubs." It shows the names of clubs that students at Maple Shade High belong to.

The height of the bars varies because the number of students in each club varies. Because the Student Council bar is the tallest bar, a viewer quickly sees that more students belong to the student council than to any other club.

The graph also shows specific information about the number of members in each club. The label on the left side of the graph, or the **vertical** axis, says "Number of Students." It shows intervals of 20. A viewer looks at the vertical axis to find out how many students belong to each club. For example, the bar that represents the photography club members stops halfway between the line marked 20 and the line marked 40. This means that the photography club has 30 members.

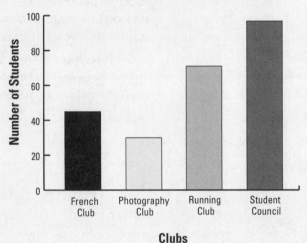

Maple Shade High Club Membership

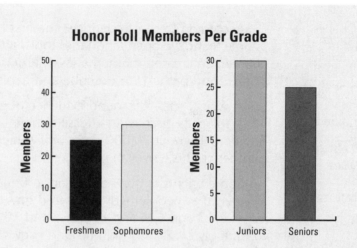

Honor Roll Members Per Grade

The information in the graphs above is misleading. At first, it appears that the number of juniors who made the honor roll was more than the number of sophomores who did. However, look carefully at the vertical **axes**. The unequal scales cause the misreading. A viewer should always carefully compare the increments on the scales of a graph. This will reduce the chances of receiving false information.

Sometimes, graphs are intended to mislead. Advertisers try to convince viewers that a certain product is "the best." A misleading graph can show that one product is much less expensive—or more successful—than another product. A viewer who receives this false information is more likely to buy the advertised product.

Be sure to check the graphs you read. Look carefully at the data for a clearer picture.

Vocabulary Tip

Some technical terms form their plurals in different ways. Here, you'll see the word *axes*. *Axes* is the plural of *axis*.

Math History:
Early Mathematics

Vocabulary Tip

A definition of *tallies* appears between commas immediately after the word.

According to most scientists, the first humans lived in Africa. There, people first developed language, tools, and organized ways of living. People also created mathematics. Mathematics is the use of numbers, shapes, and patterns to describe and explain the world.

In Africa, scientists found evidence of early people's use of math. Archaeologists discovered a fossil bone in a place called Ishango in Zaire. The bone is about 20,000 years old. **Tallies**, or marks that represent number counts, cover the bone.

Some scientists think the Ishango bone was a calendar. Others think it shows that people had discovered how to multiply. They believe the tallies for 3 and 6, 4 and 8, and 5 and 10 show that people knew how to multiply by 2. Although no one knows the specific meaning of the Ishango bone, scientists do know it shows that early humans were thinking mathematically.

Tallies are one way to write numbers. People use tallies to count days or objects. However, using tallies to record numbers presents a problem. It is difficult to write large numbers using tally marks. So people invented a new way to record numbers. Around 3100 B.C., Egyptians in the Nile Valley were using numerals.

The Egyptians still used tallies for numbers 1 through 9. For 10, they used a symbol that stood for 10 tallies. The number 11 was represented by the symbol and one tally mark. The number 12 was represented by the symbol and two tally marks. The Egyptians invented more symbols to write numbers up to 1,000,000. The symbols made representing large numbers much easier. Modern numerals reflect that idea of using symbols instead of tallies.

The Nile Valley dwellers also created a system of measures. They needed a system to figure out fair exchanges in the marketplace. The Egyptians used the length of a forearm to measure cloth. They called that length a cubit. However, problems arose because people's arms are different lengths. A short arm was good for the seller. A long arm was good for the buyer. To make a trade, the buyer and the seller had to agree on the length of the cubit. The Egyptians decided a cubit would be the length of the forearm of the pharaoh or king. That made the cubit a standard length.

We can also trace fractions to the ancient Egyptians. To measure fractions of a cubit, they used palms and fingers. Four fingers equaled one palm, and seven palms equaled one cubit. For fine measures, fingers were divided into halves, thirds, fourths, and so on.

The Egyptians made the first calendar that had 365 days in one year.

The first mathematical ideas were developed without the aid of modern technology. Early Egyptian mathematicians lived thousands of years ago and had few tools to work with. However, their ideas serve as a basis for mathematical ideas used by present-day people.

Vocabulary Tip

Illusion is defined in this paragraph. Why might Thomas have called her invention an *illusion transmitter*?

Suppose that you are watching a television show. Suddenly, a character jumps out of the TV screen and into the room. He seems to be next to you, but you can't touch him. When you try, your hand goes right through him.

According to Valerie Thomas, that is the future of TV. In 1980, she received a patent for a device she invented. She calls her invention an "illusion transmitter." An **illusion** is something that isn't real but seems to be. Thomas's illusion transmitter uses special mirrors. The mirrors create a 3-D image that you can see without special glasses.

Not a Proper Subject for a Girl

No one who knew Thomas as a child was surprised when she became an inventor. Electronics had always interested her. However, many people in the 1940s thought that electronics was not a proper subject for girls.

Thomas had done activities form *The Boy's First Book of Electronics* before age nine. Her all-girls school, though, didn't give her a chance to tinker. Thomas stayed away from electronics—for a while.

Thomas did very well in math all through school. However, she didn't take any advanced math classes. The courses weren't required, and her friends weren't taking them. That was "the most fatal mistake I made in high school," she says. When she went to college, Thomas had to take calculus in her second year. She had only one year to catch up.

Thomas attended Morgan State University in Baltimore, Maryland. At Morgan, she was one of only two women in her class studying physics. After graduation, Thomas studied computer science. She earned a master's degree in engineering administration from George Washington University in Washington, D.C.

Thomas Works at NASA

Thomas worked at NASA's Goddard Space Flight Center for 31 years. She made computer data systems that helped to control spacecraft. She also managed a team that used NASA's first scientific computer network. That network linked thousands of space-research computers. Her work helped scientists studying Earth, stars, Halley's comet, the hole in Earth's ozone layer, and the planets Neptune and Uranus. The network helped scientists all over the world to exchange information.

Vocabulary Tip

Satellites are machines that orbit planets and send back data. What do you think a satellite could tell people about Earth and the other planets?

Much of Thomas's work involved satellites. **Satellites** are machines that orbit planets. They send back data about the solar system and the Milky Way galaxy. Thomas helped develop computer data systems to interpret the information from these satellites. The data provided valuable information about world climates, the sun, Earth's oceans, and other planets.

Helping Young People See the Future

Thomas retired from NASA in 1995. She left so that she could spend more time working on her illusion transmitter. She hopes that one day everyone will receive 3-D images through their TVs.

Throughout her career, Thomas has helped guide young people into technical fields. She develops programs that are designed to interest female and minority students in technology. She wants to send them a message: You can succeed in any area—if you try.

Computer Science: Sharing With Our Neighbors

Kenneth A. Granderson has always liked to explore new ideas. When his high school got its first computer, Granderson gave it a try. "With computers, I found I could explore almost anything," he says. Granderson later turned his passion for computers into a career.

Granderson creates computer software, the programs that people use with their computers. His company is called ICS (Inner-City Software). The name hints at more than the company's location. It is a clue to Granderson's greatest mission.

Finding the Perfect Fit

Kenneth Granderson grew up in a poor section of Brooklyn, New York. He worked hard in high school. On Saturdays and during summers, he attended computer classes for teens held at a local college. Granderson's hard work earned him entrance to MIT (Massachusetts Institute of Technology) in Boston, Massachusetts. He majored in electrical engineering.

Granderson's studies at MIT "taught me how to tackle big and complex problems," he says. "You need this skill to develop software." Granderson graduated from MIT in 1985. He went to work for a large company, testing software made by other people. Then he began to write his own programs. He started ICS in 1992.

A Universe of Possibilities

ICS is based in Dorchester, Massachusetts. Dorchester is a section of Boston where many African Americans and people from other minority groups live. Most Dorchester families have little money. ICS has clients all over the world, but the people Granderson really wants to reach are right in his neighborhood.

Granderson urges people who live in poorer areas of cities to use computers. He believes technology can improve the lives of poorer people. Computers can link people to the world outside their neighborhoods. They offer **access** to an endless flow of ideas and information. Technology "can open up a universe of possibilities," Granderson says.

Vocabulary Tip

The word *access* means "a way or means of entering."

If people who live in poorer areas can benefit from these possibilities, what keeps kids in big cities from using computers? Granderson thinks one problem is a lack of programs that appeal to city kids. He is trying to change that. He plans to develop as much software geared to big-city teenagers as he can. His first project was about the history of African Americans in Boston. He also led a major Internet project. The Internet is a network that links computers around the world. It allows the people in Dorchester to "share our creative output with our neighbors and the world."

The number of people who use computers grows every day. Kenneth Granderson wants kids to be part of that trend. He wants kids to look beyond their neighborhoods and use computers to see what the world might have to offer them.

Kenneth Granderson